Dedication

To Joe. What a joy doing life together!

Acknowledgments

Thanks first to Wendy Keller of ForthWrite Literary Agency for calling me in January, 1996 to ask if I'd ever considered writing a book on copyright.

I would like to thank the many staff members who have been part of The Permissions Group over the years, without whose support and encouragement I would accomplish very little: Sherry, Lin, Joe, Stephanie, Mary Ann, Lynn, Linda, Val, Dorothy, Jan, Susanne, Jennifer, Melissa, Claudia, Rori, Samantha, Celeste, Liz, Jennifer M., Mary M., Mary C., Megan, Eileen, Anita, Sara, Jean, plus our honorary Board Members Ruth and Marge, as well as Kate, the original TPG Baby.

Many thanks to my original copyright mentors, Barbara Bartolotta and Robert Ravas. I owe much gratitude to those who have helped me to develop and hone my copyright knowledge and skills, including everyone who contacted me with questions after reading the first edition of *Copyright Plain & Simple,* those who have attended my seminars and training sessions on copyright, all who sent me questions via *copyRights©* or our website, as well as the many, many clients we've worked with at The Permissions Group. You've all kept me sharp and helped me to help you!

Finally, this second edition of *Copyright Plain & Simple* has been set in type with the support and encouragement of the folks at Career Press, including my publisher Ron Fry, my editor Jodi Brandon, and Mike Gaffney and Kirsten Beucler in marketing.

Copyright
Plain&Simple

Second Edition
Cheryl Besenjak

CAREER
PRESS
Franklin Lakes, NJ

Copyright © 2001 by Cheryl Besenjak

COPYRIGHT PLAIN & SIMPLE
Cover design by Barry Littman
Printed in the U.S.A. by Book-mart Press

To order this title, please call toll-free 1-800-CAREER-1 (NJ and Canada: 201-848-0310) to order using VISA or MasterCard, or for further information on books from Career Press.

CAREER PRESS

The Career Press, Inc., 3 Tice Road, PO Box 687,
Franklin Lakes, NJ 07417
www.careerpress.com

Library of Congress Cataloging-in-Publication Data

Besenjak, Cheryl, 1949-
    Copyright plain & simple / by Cheryl Besnjak.— 2nd ed.
        p. cm. — (Plain & simple series)
    Rev. ed. of: Copyright plain and simple. c1997.
    Includes index.
    ISBN 1-56414-512-3 (pbk.)
        1. Copyright—United States—Popular works. I. Title: Copyright plain and simple. II. Besenjak, Cheryl, 1949- Copyright plain and simple. III. Title. IV. Series.

    KF2995 .B47 2000
    346.7304'82—dc21

                                                    00-046594

Contents

Contents (cont.)

Preface

ver since I started my copyright consulting company, a number of people have asked me the same question: "Is there a really good book on copyright?" Until the publication of this book, I didn't have a good answer for them—not because there weren't any books with useful information on copyright. There are several.

But I knew what these folks were really looking for. Most of them had a number of basic questions about copyright. The majority of the books had more information than the average reader needed to know (or any attorney, for that matter) about the subject.

These people had questions such as, "How do I get a copyright for my poem?" "If something is really old it's in the public domain, right?" "How do I get permission to use copyright-protected material and when do I need to get it?" "If I change the words a little, is it fair use?" "What *is* fair use?"

The fact was, there were no "really good books on copyright." Not the kind these folks were looking for—something that would speak to their everyday questions.

Enter Wendy Keller of ForthWrite Literary Agency. Wendy had seen a copy of my newsletter called **copyRights**©

and was wondering if I had ever considered writing a book. I told her I had, but that I was busy with my rights and permissions consulting company and the newsletter. The book would have to wait a few years.

After she and I discussed the matter for a while and I related all the requests I had received for a "really good book on copyright," Wendy finally convinced me that sooner was better than later, and that giving one more job to a busy person was one of the best ways to get it done.

As I put together my vision for *Copyright Plain & Simple,* I recalled a "life experience." My husband, Joe, had the opportunity to see the Reverend Jesse Jackson speak at Operation PUSH in Chicago. As Rev. Jackson delivered his message, Joe was taken by one phrase that some members of the audience shouted out during Jackson's speech: "Make it plain, Jesse. Make it plain." As this book was taking shape, this phrase continued to resonate in my mind. And I knew that I was being called upon to "make it plain."

The electronic age has made us all creators and users of copyright material—whether we realize it or not. Whether you are a college student honing your computer skills by creating a home page on the World Wide Web, a freelance desktop publisher building your business, or a songwriter creating digital music, you definitely have a need to know about copyright. The mission of *Copyright Plain & Simple* is to make copyright plain—to take the law, boil it down, and apply it to our everyday lives through everyday examples.

And although my goal is to simplify the law for you, the truth is that the law can be complex and each copyright situation can bring its own unique set of circumstances. I believe that *Copyright Plain & Simple* will serve as a valuable resource for explaining copyright basics, answering everyday questions and providing a springboard when your copyright situation goes beyond plain and simple.

Chapter 1

Copyright Affects Everyone

You search your garage in a panic. You can't find the cassette tape containing your favorite obscure recording of Connie Francis singing "Where the Boys Are." You've tried to find it on CD with no luck. Just before you give up hope, a friend tells you about a new Web site that gives you access to an almost unlimited number of songs, even hard-to-find ones, for free! You go to the site, download the software, and find your song.

You thank your friend for helping to get you and Connie back together again. Your friend tells you about all the free music that's available on the site. In fact, your friend hasn't bought a CD in a long time. You ask why. The friend tells you that not only can you find any song you want and copy it, but you can buy the hardware to actually "burn" your own CDs. You ask if this is legal. Your friend says that its okay because you're really just "sharing" music with other people.

©©©

You're the V.P. of Sales for a Fortune 500 company. It's your responsibility to put together the opening session for the annual sales conference in Las Vegas. You need to get the salespeople motivated and thinking about the financial rewards they can strive for in the coming year. Something immediately jumps into your mind. It's highly recognizable, very motivational, and it has to do with high earnings. You open the main session of the sales conference by showing the famous "show me the money" scene from the film *Jerry Maguire*. You achieve the desired effect. The room full of high-earners can think of nothing but the money they will earn. After the presentation, a fellow executive commends you on a job well done. She asks, "By the way, did it cost very much to get permission to show that clip?" You reply, "Permission?"

©©©

You're a college student who decides to liven up your dorm room by painting your own version of the Sistine Chapel on the ceiling. Students and professors alike applaud your creativity. Unfortunately, the university's regulations prohibit students from decorating their rooms in any way that would "mar" the walls, woodwork, doors, or furnishings. Even though the rules don't specifically address re-creating famous artworks on the ceilings, school officials inform you that the ceiling will be painted over. You decide that neither you nor your ceiling will go down without a fight, so you hire a lawyer and file suit against the school. Thanks to a 1990 amendment to the copyright law known as the Visual Artists Rights Act, you win a reprieve for your "lofty creation."

Copyright affects everyone

You may not be one of the chosen few who know the formula for Coca-Cola (trade secret), invented a cardiovascular exercise machine that revolutionizes the fitness industry (patent), or created a multibillion dollar company with a burger and two yellow arches (trademark). But anyone who has ever written a letter, snapped a photo, painted a picture, whittled a bird on the end of a walking stick, taped a favorite show from television, or sung "Happy Birthday" at a party is involved in copyright.

Today, with computers in a steadily growing number of households, anyone can be a desktop publisher. Whether we are creating a newsletter for a scout troop, collecting our mother's favorite recipes to be bound as a family gift, designing greeting cards to be sold at a Christmas boutique, or writing a book, copyright is indeed part of our everyday lives.

Copyright is big business. In its 1999 report, The International Intellectual Property Alliance stated that, for the eighth straight year, copyright industries continue to be one of the fastest growing segments of the U.S. economy. In 1997, the core copyright industries (those industries that create copyrighted works as their primary product) contributed an estimated $348.4 billion to the U.S. economy, accounting for approximately 4.3 percent of the gross domestic product.

The U.S. government has exhibited an understanding of the importance of copyright in today's electronic age. In February 1993, President Clinton formed the Information Infrastructure Task Force to study the impact of the National Information Infrastructure (otherwise known as the electronic superhighway) and to update the law on copyright if necessary. The Working Group on Intellectual Property Rights published its findings, titled "Intellectual Property and the National Information Infrastructure," in September 1995. Given these findings, our lawmakers have been debating legislation regarding our nation's current and future needs with regard to protecting copyrighted material while encouraging the creativity that moves us forward.

Yet ask the average person on the street what copyright is and you get a response such as, "It's that little 'c' thing with a circle that means somebody owns it." Most citizens do not understand copyright or why we need to protect it.

Perhaps this example will hit home: What if you returned from work one day and found that the maple tree in your front yard had been cut down? Or that your living room furniture was rearranged? What if someone set up a tent on your front lawn? After you recovered from the shock, you would probably take immediate steps to protect your property. You might ask the people to get off your property or call the police.

We all understand the concept of "real" (as in real estate) property. There are laws to protect "real" property; no one has the right to trespass. The same is true for "intellectual" property. No one has the right to trespass on it. This right is granted in the Copyright Act of 1976, the current copyright law.

The importance
of copyright knowledge

We would like to think that *piracy* only took place on the high seas in days gone by. Yet billions of revenue dollars are lost through piracy of copyrighted material every year. And what about *cyber*-piracy? A variety of bills have been proposed in recent years designed to protect copyrighted material on the Internet.

If creators of copyrighted material ("manufacturers") are routinely "hijacked," these creators might no longer be encouraged to create. This could hinder the goal of copyright granted in the Constitution of the United States to "promote the progress of science and useful arts." Respect for the property is important for our country to move forward intellectually and creatively.

If you are a creator of copyrighted material, it is important to understand your rights. We are deeply involved in a technological revolution. Information is sent or received around the world with one click of a mouse. Old photos can look as though they were taken yesterday. Any student doing a research paper can type "Maya Angelou" into a search engine and download her poem, "On the Pulse of Morning," written for and recited at President Clinton's inauguration.

Because we are able to dabble with other people's intellectual property so easily, we may not even consider that the property is protected, that there is an invisible "no trespassing" sign on it or a fence around it.

It is everyone's responsibility to know the law and understand its application in all media so that we can make responsible and intelligent decisions about the way we use other people's property.

The cost of *not* understanding copyright protection could be high. Just ask George Frena. In 1993, Playboy Enterprises sued cybervendor Frena for transmitting digitized images of *Playboy* photographs. Although Frena removed the images whenever his customers transmitted them onto his system, a court found Frena liable for infringing on Playboy Enterprise's copyrights and trademarks. ("Playboy" and "Playmate" are registered trademarks.) Even though these were instances of "innocent" infringement, Frena was liable.

It is essential to fully understand copyright law and its application to our real lives as we sit down to write a term paper, create "Grandma's Best Recipes," or take our photos to be restored. Use *Copyright Plain & Simple* to make a sometimes-complex law understandable. Then you can explain to the camera store employee that because your family photos were "published" before 1923, they are out of copyright and in the public domain. Permission is no longer needed from the studio (if the studio was indeed the copyright holder) and the photos are free for anyone to use and reproduce.

A look at what you'll learn

You come into contact with copyright law much more often than you realize. Whether you're writing a book or creating your church bulletin, you're involved in copyright.

Here's a brief list of the questions we'll explore in *Copyright Plain & Simple*:

© What is copyright, and why is it important?

© What is an "intellectual property," and how is it similar to other types of property?

© When did copyright law start, and how has it changed over the years?

© What types of properties are protected by copyright, and what types aren't?

© How are books, magazines, and other forms of the printed word protected by copyright?

© Does copyright for visual works of art such as paintings and photographs differ from other types of copyright?

© Can a performance such as a play, a ballet, or a speech be protected by copyright?

© What copyright issues should be considered when it comes to music?

© How has the Internet affected copyright?

© What do you need to know about copyright and photocopying?

© How do you know who holds the rights to an intellectual property, and how do you get permission to use it?

© What is "fair use," and when can you claim it?

© What constitutes copyright infringement, and how can you avoid it?

© What special copyright concerns do libraries and educational institutions face?

© With all the changes in technology, what does the future hold for copyright law?

Whether you are dealing with the printed word, visual arts, music, film, the Internet, theater, or software, this book will give you practical applications of the law. It will help you to protect your own intellectual properties as well as minimize your risk of liability when using properties that belong to others. In other words, this book will be an invaluable guide that explains copyright *plain and simple.*

Chapter 2

What is Copyright?

I f you came home from work one day and found that your prize rose bushes had been cut to the ground or your garage door was sporting a new coat of pink latex, you would be on the phone to the police immediately.

Real vs. intellectual property

We are all aware of our rights as "real" property owners. No one has the right to come onto our property and, certainly, no one has the right to deface or destroy it. There are laws to protect our property and we know our rights.

But let's say that you have written a historical novel based on the life and times of Napoleon Bonaparte. Soon after your novel is published you see a movie on HBO that bears a striking resemblance to your work. You should be on the phone to an attorney as fast as you can say "derivative work!"

Real property and intellectual property have much in common. Intellectual property may not be something you can put your arms around, but it exists and has value. Time and effort may have gone into its creation and shape. No one should have the right to trespass on or deface it. Just as real property is protected by law, so is intellectual property protected by law: *copyright* law.

Copyright roots

The foundations of U.S. copyright law were laid down more than 300 years ago in England. With the advent and popularity of printing technology, the intellectual property of others became more accessible. Before the printing press, the *pirating* of another's work required the investment of a great deal of time and effort. Was it worth all that time and effort to make one copy?

The invention of the printing press raised new issues. With it, an author's work could be reproduced quickly and at much less expense—which meant a greater audience and greater revenue—for *someone*. Paul Goldstein addresses the issues this new technology raised in *Copyright's Highway*:

> "Who should be entitled to share in the newly opened cache of literary value? The author who created the text? The publisher who financed the risk that copies of the text might never find enough readers to repay the cost of printing and distributing it? Or—once author and publisher were paid—the public, in the form of lower prices?"[1]

In 1557, 80 years after William Caxton brought the printing press to England, a royal charter was granted to a guild of scribes, printers, bookbinders, and booksellers. For the next few hundred years, the Stationers' Company controlled the rights to writings. These rights were passed down through the generations, in perpetuity. Writers were paid lump sums for their work and had no rights thereafter. The Stationers' Company had a monopoly on the publishing business. It was truly an era of "publisher's rights."

---

[1]Paul Goldstein, *Copyright's Highway*. New York: Hill and Wang, 1994, p. 40.

The Statute of Anne (1709)

The Crown of England was anxious to control the words that came off the press. A variety of censorship acts led to the Licensing Act of 1662. This act originally had a two-year term but was renewed continually.

Resentment mounted regarding the monopoly and powers of censorship of the Stationers' Company. In 1709, this monopoly was broken when Parliament refused to renew the Licensing Act of 1662 and with the enactment of the Statute of Anne. No longer was it a violation of the stationers' copyright to publish a work.

The Statute of Anne was written as an "[a]ct for the encouragement of learning, by vesting the copies of printed books in the authors or purchasers of such copies, during the times therein mentioned." The statute provided copyright protection to the author for a term of 28 years. Thus began the period of "author's rights."

The first U.S. Law (1790)

The Statute of Anne, carried across the Atlantic Ocean by English colonists, underwent testing and evolution that continued after the colonies won independence from England. As a result of lobbying by writers such as Noah Webster and Thomas Paine, its concepts were incorporated into early state copyright laws.

The U.S. Congress articulated its idea of copyright by using the following language: "The Congress shall have power...to promote the progress of science and useful arts, by securing for limited times to authors and inventors the exclusive right to their respective writings and discoveries." On May 31, 1790, President George Washington signed into effect the first national Copyright Act, granting a 14-year term of copyright protection for books, maps, and charts. On June 9, 1790 the first copyrighted work was registered in the U.S. District Court of Pennsylvania: *The Philadelphia Spelling Book* by John Barry.

The Copyright Act of 1909

Over the years other technologies have tested and changed the U.S. law. Music gained copyright protection in 1831, dramatic compositions were added in 1856, and photography became copyrightable in 1865, presumably due to Mathew Brady, the famous Civil War photographer.

The player piano brought about a significant change in the law. Apollo, a manufacturer of player pianos, was sued by White-Smith Music Publishing Co. for copyright infringement in 1908. Although printed music was protected by copyright, recorded music was not. Player pianos raised the question of whether paper with holes was a "copy" of musical notation. Composers Victor Herbert and John Philip Sousa testified in favor of protection. The copyright law was revised, and the Copyright Act of 1909 was enacted.

The Copyright Act of 1976

The first 70 years of the 20th century has been called the Era of Communications. The phonograph, radio, television, photocopier, video camera, and computers were all introduced during this time. Until the late 1970s, copyright law only protected those works that were *published,* with publication defined as the distribution of copies of a work to the public by sale or other transfer of ownership, or by rental, lease, or lending. The offering to distribute copies of a work to a group of people for the purposes of further distribution, public performance, or public display also constitutes publication.

William S. Strong interprets the legal definition of publication in *The Copyright Book: A Practical Guide*:

> "The concept of publication has been crucial to copyright law from the beginning. Publication is the act of offering copies to the public. There does not have to be an actual distribution. Even if there is a distribution, it does not have to be a sale; giving copies away

to the public is sufficient. The size of the public is irrelevant; handing out one or two copies can constitute publication. And though performance or display of a work is not publication in and of itself, distributing copies to a group of persons who will themselves perform or display the work does not count as publication, unless those persons are your employees or otherwise act under your control."[2]

In 1976, revisions were proposed that meant that creators no longer needed to publish a work for it to be copyrighted. Copyright was immediate—at creation. Thus began an era of greater author's rights. This revision was enacted January 1, 1978, although the name of the act remains the Copyright Act of 1976. It remains our current law for the protection of copyrighted property.

What is copyrightable?

Copyright law lists the following types of works of authorship as those that can be protected by copyright:

© Literary works.

© Musical works, including any accompanying words.

© Dramatic works, including any accompanying music.

© Pantomimes and choreographic works.

© Pictorial, graphic, and sculptural works.

© Motion pictures and other audiovisual works.

© Sound recordings.

© Architectural works.

---

[2]William S. Strong, *The Copyright Book: A Practical Guide, Fourth Edition.* Cambridge, Mass.: The MIT Press, 1994, p. 78.

What is not copyrightable?

The following are *not* protected by copyright law in the United States: (Although some may be protected by trademark or patent law or possibly by laws prohibiting unfair competition, they are not copyrightable.)

© Works that are not in a fixed form of expression. For example, choreographic works that have not been notated or recorded, extemporaneous speeches or improvisational performances that are not written or recorded.

© Titles, names, short phrases, and slogans (these may be protected by trademark law).

© Familiar symbols or designs—such as "smiley faces" and no-smoking signs.

© Type fonts, lettering, or coloring.

© Ideas, procedures, methods, systems, processes, concepts, principles, discoveries, or devices.

© Works consisting entirely of information that is common property and containing no original authorship. For example: standard calendars; height and weight charts; tape measures and rulers; lists or tables taken from public documents or other common sources.

The requirements of copyright

Copyright protection is awarded to works of authorship that:

© Are original.

© Exhibit minimal creativity.

© Are fixed in a tangible form of expression. (Fixed form is defined as a form that can preserve the work so that it can be read back or heard, either directly or with the aid of a machine.)

The more creative the work, and the more you can prove your work is unique, the more likely your work will be granted protection. Start with a stick figure drawing and there may not be much to copyright. But add a plaid scarf and a beret, give the figure a name, and you are on your way to creating a copyrightable character.

What are the *exclusive rights* granted by law to copyrighted works? According to Section 106 of Title 17 of the United States Code, the following rights in copyrighted works are protected. The copyright owner has the *exclusive rights* to and authorizes others to:

©   Reproduce the work.

©   Prepare derivative works of the work.

©   Distribute copies of the work.

©   Perform the work publicly.

©   Display the work publicly.

What is a reproduction?

One of the exclusive rights of a copyright holder is the right to make copies of or reproduce a protected work. Here are examples of reproductions of copyrighted works:

©   A photocopy of a magazine article.

©   An extra set of prints from your roll of film.

©   A photograph that has been scanned into a computer.

©   A print copy of an e-mail message.

©   A copy of a cassette.

©   A backup of a computer disk.

What is a derivative work?

The copyright owner has the exclusive right to create adaptations of a protected work and transform the protected work into a new work. The following are examples of derivative works:

© A screenplay from a novel.

© A painting from a photo.

© A postcard from a painting.

© A rap song from a rock song.

© A puzzle created from a photo.

© A fabric pattern from a graphic design.

© A ballad from a poem.

What is distribution?

The following are examples of ways in which a copyrighted work might be distributed:

© Passing out pamphlets on a street corner.

© Sending an article to clients.

© Publishing and selling a book throughout the world.

© Sending an e-mail message to another person in a company.

© Displaying brochures in a rack on a store counter.

© Mailing a flyer to residents in a particular area.

What is a public performance?

A public performance of a copyrighted work is another right that the copyright owner holds. Here are a few examples of performances:

©   Acting on a stage.

©   Singing in a club.

©   Making a recording.

©   Showing a movie in a theater.

©   Broadcasting a sports event.

What is a public display?

A copyright holder has the exclusive right to publicly display a copyrighted work. Here are some examples protected by copyright law:

©   Posting the work on a bulletin board.

©   Hanging a print on the wall of a library.

©   Displaying the work on a classroom computer screen.

©   Exhibiting a painting at an art gallery.

©   Placing a sculpture in the lobby of a building.

Two key copyright concepts

1. Ideas are not copyrightable! The idea of a "four-bedroom house" can mean different things to different people. That idea is not copyrightable. What is copyrightable is the *expression* of the idea "four-bedroom house." The architect designs the floor plans for the house, a writer describes the house in a short story, a photographer captures the house in the late-afternoon sun, a painter renders a watercolor vision of the house, a lyricist writes a ballad about the house, and so on. Each artist has portrayed the idea of a "four-bedroom house" through a different form of expression. It is this expression, this unique way of expressing the idea, that is copyrightable.

2. Facts are not copyrightable! Let's say you are driving to the coffee shop down the street. You see a car swerve off the road, hit a fence, and knock down a mailbox. You stop your car to check on the driver, who appears to have some minor cuts and bruises but is in good spirits. Speaking of spirits, you do smell alcohol. As you call the police department on your cell phone to report this, you note that your watch says it is 1:30 p.m. The facts in this sequence of events are not copyrightable in and of themselves. But a news story about the events written by a reporter for the local paper *is* copyrightable. In other words, neither you nor anyone else has the exclusive right to tell the story about the incident. Once the story is told by the news reporter or TV commentator, though, that expression of the story as related by the reporter or commentator is protected by copyright.

Transferring copyright

Just as with any real property, any or all of the exclusive rights—and any subdivision of those rights—involving an intellectual property can be bought, sold, and transferred. A homeowner can sell his home, rent it, donate it to an organization, or will it to his children. So can an artist transfer his intellectual property in the same manner.

Because these rights are exclusive to the owner, the transfer must be conveyed by contractual agreement *in writing*. You wouldn't think of letting someone rent your house for a year without a lease. What if the tenants burned a hole in the carpeting? What if they had 10 friends move in right away? What if they never paid their rent? Just as with real property, it is important to spell out (in writing) all expectations and restrictions regarding intellectual property.

Types of transfers

Transfers of any or all rights in an author's copyright should not be taken lightly. It is a contractual arrangement. The following are types of transfers:

1. **Exclusive license.** A transfer of one or more of the rights of a copyright holder.

2. **Nonexclusive license.** A transfer allowing someone the right to exercise one or more of the rights on a nonexclusive basis. This is not a transfer of copyright ownership.

3. **Assignment.** A transfer of all the exclusive rights in a copyright.

A transfer of copyright ownership must be in writing to be valid. It is also a good idea to record an all-rights transfer, an *assignment*, with the Copyright Office. The assignment is then a matter of public record. The process is similar to recording a deed with the county in which you reside.

What are subsidiary rights?

Your property can be *subdivided*. The rights that protect portions of the property are called subsidiary rights.

An example of subsidiary rights can be found in virtually any book publishing contract between an author and a publisher. The primary right in a literary work is the right of publication. When an author signs a contract, he or she is granting to the publisher the right to print copies of the work and distribute the copies to be sold. All other rights are the subsidiary rights. These can include:

© Printing paperback editions (or hardbound editions if the contract is for paperback).

© Selling the work to be made into a movie, TV show, play, or radio series.

© Publishing all or part of the work in a newspaper, magazine, or other periodical.

© Making or selling foreign translations of the work.

© Making audio recordings of a literary work (a book or poem).

© Electronic rights.

Subsidiary rights are negotiable and valuable. If you have written a book, for example, you may want to retain rights for foreign translations, audio recordings, or electronic rights of your work. Be sure you understand what rights you have, what rights you want, and what rights you are willing to give away.

What is a work for hire?

When is the creator of an intellectual property *not* the owner of the copyright? When the work is created in a work-for-hire situation. Although the Copyright Act of 1976 states that copyright protection begins at creation and when a work is in a fixed form, it also defines two situations in which the creator of a work does not have the rights to the work.

The first situation is when an employee performs or creates work for his employer within the scope of the employee's job description. This is an understood agreement between the two parties. No written agreement is necessary. What constitutes a work made by an employee? The kind of work the employee is asked to perform. It occurs during the employee's work hours. It is performed to serve the employer.

For example, a copywriter for an ad agency is hired to write text for advertising. Therefore, if that employee creates a brochure while working there, it is the agency's right to profit from that work—not the creator of the brochure.

The second situation is when the work is considered a work for hire. When a company or individual commissions work by an author, copyright ownership clearly rests with the commissioning party if the agreement between the two parties is in writing. The following are types of commissioned works that are considered to be works for hire under the Copyright Act of 1976.

©   A contribution to a collective work.

©   Part of a motion picture or other audiovisual work, such as a screenplay.

©   A translation.

©   A supplementary work prepared as an adjunct to a work prepared by another person, such as a foreword, index, appendix, chart, illustration, map, or bibliography.

©   A compilation.

©   An instructional text.

©   A test or answer key.

©   An atlas.

Who is the author in a work-for-hire situation? For copyright purposes, the employer or the party who commissions the work is the author of the work and, thus, the copyright holder. This copyright holder can be a person or an entity, such as a company.

An important note: In order for a contractual agreement to be valid, a work-for-hire agreement must be signed *before* the work begins.

Negotiating a contract

Whether you are writing the great American novel, creating an index for a textbook, or drawing a cartoon strip for your local paper, it is essential that you understand your rights. Before signing any contractual agreement, understand what you are keeping or giving away. A good resource for understanding publishing law is *Kirsch's Handbook of Publishing Law* by Jonathan Kirsch (see Appendix A). If you are not sure about the language, have an attorney review your contract. You could be giving away valuable rights!

Edgar Rice Burroughs, the creator of Tarzan, clearly understood the importance of property rights. In his article "Protecting the Author's Rights," which he wrote for *The Writers 1932 Year Book & Market Guide,* he cautioned authors: "Watch all of your rights all of the time; they are the basis of your entire literary estate." Your property (be it real or intellectual) has great value. Enjoy the protection you are granted under the law.

Summary

Copyright protects intellectual property, just as other laws protect real property. Pertinent parts of the Copyright Act are reprinted in Appendix C in this book. Here are some highlights regarding the origins and foundations of copyright law:

©   U.S. copyright law existed before the country did—with the Statute of Anne in England in 1709.

©   The U.S. copyright law is founded in the Constitution, Article I, Section 8.

©   The first U.S. Copyright Act was signed into law by George Washington on May 31, 1790.

©   The next major change in copyright came with the Copyright Act of 1909, as a result of an infringement suit over player pianos.

©   The Copyright Act of 1976 is the current copyright law that governs us.

©   Current copyright law grants a copyright holder the following exclusive rights:

    1. The right to reproduce the work.

    2. The right to prepare derivative works.

    3. The right to distribute copies of the work.

    4. The right to perform the work publicly.

    5. The right to display the work publicly.

©   It is the buying and selling of these rights that give intellectual property economic value.

©   Ideas are not copyrightable.

©   Facts are not copyrightable.

©   When negotiating a contract that involves copyright issues, be aware of the rights you are keeping and those you are selling (or giving away).

Chapter 3

Copyright Basics

D espite the title of this book, most people don't think of copyright as simple. Although copyright *can* be quite perplexing, if you learn the basics, you will have the tools to view each copyright situation appropriately and apply a foundation of knowledge to find the answers you need.

Old law and new law

There are two U.S. copyright laws you should be familiar with: the Copyright Act of 1909 and the current law, the Copyright Act of 1976.

Why is it important to be familiar with the old act? Although you are creating works under the current law, you may very well want to use works created under the old law. The current law became effective on January 1, 1978. For copyright purposes we will discuss works as having been created before 1978 or after 1978. The two laws are significantly different. One of the first questions you must ask yourself when considering use of others' material is, "What law was it created/published under?"

The Copyright Act of 1909

Under the Copyright Act of 1909, a work had to be *published* to be awarded copyright protection. In addition, the work had to have a notice of copyright, and the copyright had to have been registered. If the work was published without a valid copyright notice, it fell into the public domain. The initial term of copyright was 28 years. Copyright could be renewed for an additional term of 28 years. When the current law came into effect, the renewal term of previous copyrights was extended an additional 19 years. For this reason, the full term of copyright protection for works published under the Copyright Act of 1909 was 75 years. On October 27, 1998, The Sonny Bono Copyright Extension Act (Public Law 105-298) was enacted, which extended the renewal term of copyright for works in copyright on that date by 20 years. The new renewal term of 67 years gave a total term of protection of 95 years. In summary, here are the highlights of the old law:

© *Publication* was required for copyright protection.

© The law provided a 28-year term with a 47-year renewal term.

© The renewal term was extended to 67 years for works in copyright on October 27, 1998.

© A valid copyright notice had to appear with the work.

© The copyright had to be registered.

The Copyright Act of 1976

Under the current law, copyright protection is immediate and begins at the *creation* of an original work of authorship in a fixed, tangible means of expression.

The current Copyright Act redefines the terms of protection, as well. A single term of copyright is defined as either of the following:

© Life of the author plus 70 years for a work by an individual author or authors.

© 95 years from creation or 120 years from publication, whichever is sooner, for a company.

A copyright notice was a requirement of the Copyright Act of 1976 until March 1, 1989, when the United States adhered to the Berne Convention of International Copyright, which eliminated the need for a copyright notice as a requirement for protection. Before that time, works published without a copyright notice were not granted copyright protection under the law—and they entered the public domain. A creator of an intellectual property could correct this error of omission if he or she registered the work and made a reasonable effort to add a valid notice of copyright to all copies distributed after the omission was discovered.

Copyright registration is optional, although very desirable. It entitles the copyright holder to statutory damages and attorney fees should the holder prove copyright infringement. Before a copyright suit can begin, the copyright holder must prove a valid copyright in the work by registering the work with the Copyright Office and receiving a recorded certificate of copyright registration. Even though copyright protection is granted by law at creation and fixation and a copyright owner does have the right to tell an infringer to stop using the work, the holder *must* bring to court this "deed" (the certificate of registration) to the property.

To summarize, here are the highlights of the Copyright Act of 1976:

© *Creation* in fixed form is the key to protection.

© A single term of copyright is the life of the author plus 70 years for individuals; 95 years from publication or 120 years from creation, whichever is first, for a company.

© Notice of copyright is optional after March 1, 1989.

©   Registration of copyright is optional, although highly desirable.

Copyright renewal

Issues of renewal apply only to copyrights established prior to the enactment of the current law in 1978. Under the previous act, the copyright holder had until the end of the 28th year of the copyright term to submit a renewal application to the Copyright Office in order to receive another term. If the application was not received by December 31 of that year, the copyright for the work expired and the work fell into public domain. Copyright could not be recaptured.

The law was amended in 1992 to provide an automatic renewal. It had been discovered that only 20 percent of copyrights were renewed. This means that it can be assumed that any works published before 1964 have a 28-year term and a 47-year renewal period, now extended by 20 years for a total renewal of 67 years, if a timely filing of renewal was done. After 1964, published works have full 95-year protection.

Unpublished works

Until the Copyright Act of 1976, unpublished works were protected under common-law copyright and subject to state rather than federal law. A special provision in the new law, which protects a work at creation rather than at publication, protects works of original authorship that were unpublished before 1978 until December 31, 2002. If the work was published between January 1, 1978 and January 1, 2003, the copyright of the work cannot expire before December 31, 2047. In other words, you can get an extension of protection of an additional 45 years.

Works in the public domain in the U.S.

Created 1/1/78 or after	When work is fixed in tangible medium of expression	Life + 70 years (or, if work of coporate authorship, the shorter of 95 years from publication, or 120 years from creation)
Published before 1923	In public domain	None
Published between 1923 and the end of 1963	When published with notice	28 years + could be renewed for 47 years, now extended by 20 years for a total renewal of 67 years. If not so renewed, now in public domain
Published 1964–1977	When published with notice	28 years for first term; now automatic extension of 67 years for second term
Created before 1/1/78 but not published	1/1/78, the effective date of the 1976 Act, which eliminated common law copyright	Life + 70 years or 12/31/2002, whichever is greater
Created before 1/1/78 but published between then and 12/31/2002	1/1/78, the effective date of the Act, which eliminated common law copyright	Life + 70 years or 12/31/2047, whichever is greater

Source: *www.unc.edu/home/unclng/public-d.htm*

Copyright registration

Although the first copyright law was enacted in 1790, it was not until 1870 that the copyright functions were centralized under the Library of Congress. Until that time, registrations of copyright were recorded by clerks of U.S. District Courts. As of fiscal year 1995, more than 26 million works had been registered with the Library of Congress. In 1995 alone, more than 609,195 claims were registered.

What is involved in registering your copyrighted work? The following items must be submitted in the same package to the Copyright Office (Register of Copyrights, Library of Congress, Washington, D.C. 20559):

© A completed registration form.

© Two copies of the "best edition" of your work.

© A $30 filing fee per registration.

Why register a work? As mentioned earlier, it is a prerequisite to an infringement suit. Registration must be made in a timely fashion—within three months of the date of the first publication or before the date the copyright infringement began. For unpublished works, a copyright owner is entitled to statutory damages and attorney fees from the perpetrator only if the work was registered before the infringement occurred. If you find yourself in a hurry to register your work before a suit, the expedited registration will cost $500 in addition to the filing fee.

Anyone who has questions may call the Copyright Public Information Office at (202) 707-3000 for recorded information. Information specialists can answer questions by phone or in person Monday through Friday, 8:30 a.m. to 5 p.m. Eastern time, except federal holidays.

The Copyright Office Forms Hotline (202-707-9100) is available 24 hours a day to accept requests for specific registration application forms and for information circulars. Information is available on-line at The Copyright Office Web site (*www.loc.gov/copyright)* or by Fax-on-Demand (202-707-2600). Address written inquiries to: Library of Congress, Copyright Office, Publication Section, LM-455, 101 Independence Avenue S.E., Washington, D.C. 20559-6000.

Registration forms

Following are some of the types of registration forms to be completed. When in doubt as to what form to use, speak with an information specialist at the Copyright Office.

© **TX—Nondramatic literary works.** Used for works such as books, articles, computer programs, databases, speeches, poems, and essays.

© **PA—Performing arts.** Used for works such as plays, screenplays, multimedia works, song lyrics, and musical compositions.

© **SR—Sound recordings.** Used for registering works such as musical and dramatic recordings.

© **SE—Serial publications.** This form is used for works such as newspapers, magazines, newsletters, and other periodicals.

© **VA—Visual art.** Used for registering pictorial, graphic, and sculptural works.

What is the "best edition" of your work?

The best edition of your work is the highest-quality version of your work available at the time of registration. For example, a hardcover edition if the work is also in paperback, a final draft of your manuscript rather than the first draft, a compact disc rather than a cassette tape.

When can you send only one copy?

You must submit two copies of your work except when your work: is unpublished; is a multimedia work; was first published outside of the United States; or is advertising materials, lectures, sermons, speeches, or tests and test answers published separately from each other.

FEE CHANGES
Fees are effective through June 30, 2002. After that date, check the Copyright Office Website at www.loc.gov/copyright or call (202) 707-3000 for current fee information.

FORM TX
For a Nondramatic Literary Work
UNITED STATES COPYRIGHT OFFICE

REGISTRATION NUMBER

TX   TXU

EFFECTIVE DATE OF REGISTRATION

Month   Day   Year

DO NOT WRITE ABOVE THIS LINE. IF YOU NEED MORE SPACE, USE A SEPARATE CONTINUATION SHEET.

1

TITLE OF THIS WORK ▼

PREVIOUS OR ALTERNATIVE TITLES ▼

PUBLICATION AS A CONTRIBUTION If this work was published as a contribution to a periodical, serial, or collection, give information about the collective work in which the contribution appeared. Title of Collective Work ▼

If published in a periodical or serial give: Volume ▼   Number ▼   Issue Date ▼   On Pages ▼

2   a

NAME OF AUTHOR ▼

DATES OF BIRTH AND DEATH
Year Born ▼   Year Died ▼

Was this contribution to the work a "work made for hire"?
☐ Yes
☐ No

AUTHOR'S NATIONALITY OR DOMICILE
Name of Country
OR { Citizen of ▶
{ Domiciled in ▶

WAS THIS AUTHOR'S CONTRIBUTION TO THE WORK
Anonymous? ☐ Yes ☐ No
Pseudonymous? ☐ Yes ☐ No
If the answer to either of these questions is "Yes," see detailed instructions.

NATURE OF AUTHORSHIP Briefly describe nature of material created by this author in which copyright is claimed. ▼

NOTE

Under the law, the "author" of a "work made for hire" is generally the employer, not the employee (see instructions). For any part of this work that was "made for hire" check "Yes" in the space provided, give the employer (or other person for whom the work was prepared) as "Author" of that part, and leave the space for dates of birth and death blank.

b

NAME OF AUTHOR ▼

DATES OF BIRTH AND DEATH
Year Born ▼   Year Died ▼

Was this contribution to the work a "work made for hire"?
☐ Yes
☐ No

AUTHOR'S NATIONALITY OR DOMICILE
Name of Country
OR { Citizen of ▶
{ Domiciled in ▶

WAS THIS AUTHOR'S CONTRIBUTION TO THE WORK
Anonymous? ☐ Yes ☐ No
Pseudonymous? ☐ Yes ☐ No
If the answer to either of these questions is "Yes," see detailed instructions.

NATURE OF AUTHORSHIP Briefly describe nature of material created by this author in which copyright is claimed. ▼

c

NAME OF AUTHOR ▼

DATES OF BIRTH AND DEATH
Year Born ▼   Year Died ▼

Was this contribution to the work a "work made for hire"?
☐ Yes
☐ No

AUTHOR'S NATIONALITY OR DOMICILE
Name of Country
OR { Citizen of ▶
{ Domiciled in ▶

WAS THIS AUTHOR'S CONTRIBUTION TO THE WORK
Anonymous? ☐ Yes ☐ No
Pseudonymous? ☐ Yes ☐ No
If the answer to either of these questions is "Yes," see detailed instructions.

NATURE OF AUTHORSHIP Briefly describe nature of material created by this author in which copyright is claimed. ▼

3 a

YEAR IN WHICH CREATION OF THIS WORK WAS COMPLETED This information must be given in all cases. ◀ Year

b DATE AND NATION OF FIRST PUBLICATION OF THIS PARTICULAR WORK
Complete this information ONLY if this work has been published.
Month ▶ Day ▶ Year ▶ ◀ Nation

4

See instructions before completing this space.

COPYRIGHT CLAIMANT(S) Name and address must be given even if the claimant is the same as the author given in space 2. ▼

TRANSFER If the claimant(s) named here in space 4 is (are) different from the author(s) named in space 2, give a brief statement of how the claimant(s) obtained ownership of the copyright. ▼

APPLICATION RECEIVED
ONE DEPOSIT RECEIVED
TWO DEPOSITS RECEIVED
FUNDS RECEIVED

DO NOT WRITE HERE OFFICE USE ONLY

MORE ON BACK ▶ • Complete all applicable spaces (numbers 5–9) on the reverse side of this page.
• See detailed instructions. • Sign the form at line 8.

DO NOT WRITE HERE
Page 1 of ____ pages

EXAMINED BY	FORM TX
CHECKED BY	
☐ CORRESPONDENCE Yes	FOR COPYRIGHT OFFICE USE ONLY

DO NOT WRITE ABOVE THIS LINE. IF YOU NEED MORE SPACE, USE A SEPARATE CONTINUATION SHEET.

PREVIOUS REGISTRATION Has registration for this work, or for an earlier version of this work, already been made in the Copyright Office?

☐ Yes   ☐ No If your answer is "Yes," why is another registration being sought? (Check appropriate box.) ▼

a. ☐ This is the first published edition of a work previously registered in unpublished form.

b. ☐ This is the first application submitted by this author as copyright claimant.

c. ☐ This is a changed version of the work, as shown by space 6 on this application.

If your answer is "Yes," give: **Previous Registration Number ▶**   **Year of Registration ▶**

5

DERIVATIVE WORK OR COMPILATION

Preexisting Material Identify any preexisting work or works that this work is based on or incorporates. ▼

a 6

See instructions before completing this space.

Material Added to This Work Give a brief, general statement of the material that has been added to this work and in which copyright is claimed. ▼

b

DEPOSIT ACCOUNT If the registration fee is to be charged to a Deposit Account established in the Copyright Office, give name and number of Account.

Name ▼   **Account Number ▼**

a 7

CORRESPONDENCE Give name and address to which correspondence about this application should be sent.   Name/Address/Apt/City/State/ZIP ▼

b

Area code and daytime telephone number ▶   Fax number ▶

Email ▶

CERTIFICATION* I, the undersigned, hereby certify that I am the

Check only one ▶

☐ author

☐ other copyright claimant

☐ owner of exclusive right(s)

☐ authorized agent of _____

Name of author or other copyright claimant, or owner of exclusive right(s) ▲

of the work identified in this application and that the statements made by me in this application are correct to the best of my knowledge.

8

Typed or printed name and date ▼ If this application gives a date of publication in space 3, do not sign and submit it before that date.

_____ Date ▶ _____

Handwritten signature (X) ▼

X _____

Certificate will be mailed in window envelope to this address:

Name ▼
Number/Street/Apt ▼
City/State/ZIP ▼

YOU MUST
• Complete all necessary spaces
• Sign your application in space 8

SEND ALL 3 ELEMENTS IN THE SAME PACKAGE:

1. Application form
2. Nonrefundable filing fee in check or money order payable to *Register of Copyrights*
3. Deposit material

MAIL TO:
Library of Congress
Copyright Office
101 Independence Avenue, S.E.
Washington, D.C. 20559-6000

As of July 1, 1999, the filing fee for Form TX is $30.

9

How must you pay your fee?

Send a check or money order in the amount of $30 (made payable to Register of Copyrights) with your copies and completed form. If you have more than 12 transactions, you may establish a deposit account. Your fees will then be deducted at the time of transaction. To open a deposit account, obtain Circular R5 from the Copyright Office, complete the application form, and submit $250.

Searching the Copyright Office records

One way of checking the copyright status of a work is to search the Copyright Office records. These records are available to the public and may be searched in several ways. You can search the records yourself. Hours for searching are 8:30 a.m. to 5 p.m. Eastern time, Monday through Friday, except federal holidays. You can also have the Copyright Office do a search for you. There is a fee for this search, and it will take approximately eight to 12 weeks to receive a response. There are also independent search firms, located in Washington, D.C., who will perform the search for you. If you are in a hurry to get information, this may be the way to go. An independent search firm can provide you with a report within a week. Of course, the fee for this expedited service will be higher than that of the Copyright Office. One such firm is Thomson & Thomson, 1750 K Street NW, Suite 200, Washington, D.C. 20006-2305 (800-692-8833; *www.thomson-thomson.com*).

Notice of copyright

The notice of copyright—which generally includes the familiar encircled "c"—should always include the year of publication and the name of the copyright holder. It's like putting your name on the mailbox or hanging your shingle out. The copyright notice was once a requirement for copyright protection by law. However, in March 1989 the United States adopted the Berne Convention Treaty rule and eliminated the notice of copyright as a requirement for copyright protection.

Although the notice is not required, it is highly recommended. Consider it your "No Trespassing" sign for those who might be thinking of coming onto your property. While most people know they don't have a right to use your property, the sign sends a stronger message that you won't tolerate trespassing. The notice of copyright thus sends a message that you are fully aware of your rights.

What are the elements of a copyright notice? For a copyright notice to be valid, it must contain the following three elements:

© The symbol © (the letter "c" in a circle), the word "Copyright," or the abbreviation "Copr."

© The year in which the work was published.

© The name of the copyright owner.

Here are three examples of a copyright notice:

1. Copyright 1997 The Permissions Group.

2. © 1997 The Permissions Group.

3. Copr. 1997 The Permissions Group.

What is the public domain?

"The public domain is like a vast national park...without a guide for the lost traveler...or clearly defined roads," says M. William Krasilovsky in *The Business of Music.* There is a wealth of intellectual property free for the taking.

When the Statute of Anne broke the monopoly of the Stationers' Company's copyrights in 1709, one of the results was the creation of the public domain. Copyright was no longer in perpetuity. Once the term of copyright expired, the work was free for anyone to use. What types of creative works are not protected by copyright?

©   Works with expired copyrights.

©   Works consisting solely of facts or ideas.

©   Works created by United States government officials or printed by the Government Printing Office.

Because these works are free for anyone to use in any way they choose, they can be a valuable commodity. Because the material can be adapted, it proves to be a good source for a great deal of newly copyrighted works. Consider how many film versions have been produced based on Louisa May Alcott's *Little Women* or Shakespeare's *Romeo and Juliet,* and how many cartoons and movies have been created by Disney from public domain fables and fairy tales such as "Beauty and the Beast" and "Aladdin."

When looking for public domain material to exploit and create your own copyrights, you need to be aware of a few things:

1. Know where you will be distributing your works.

Understand the copyright laws present in other countries if you'll be distributing outside of the United States. Foreign law can be quite confusing, and works may have different copyright status in different countries.

For example, you may want to reprint "The Lake Isle of Innisfree" by W.B. Yeats in a novella you are writing. Although the poem was part of an 1893 collection of his work, it is in copyright in the United States. Permission to use the poem would come from the poet's publisher, Scribner. However, if you are distributing the work outside the United States, you will want to know that Yeats' works that were published during his lifetime are in the public domain in Canada. However, throughout the European Union his works are still in copyright until 2009. (Yeats died in 1939. Protection in Europe is the life of the author plus 70 years.)

2. Be careful of translations and retellings.

Works in the public domain that have been translated or retold may have a new copyright and require permission.

There may be many retellings of Aesop's Fables. It is not true that a fable is a fable is a fable. Check the copyright notice of these works and determine what is in copyright.

3. Be careful of introductory material, editorial notes, or changes.

Whenever new material is added to a public domain work, that new material may well be in copyright. Any special editing or changes to the material may also be granted copyright protection. Examples: Robert Kimbrough's preface to the Norton Critical Edition of Joseph Conrad's *Heart of Darkness*, or the explanatory footnotes in the Riverside editions of Shakespeare's "Macbeth."

Out of the public domain?

Two changes in legislation throughout the world have made it even more difficult to determine the copyright status of works.

©   In England, the term of copyright was extended from "life plus 50 years" to "life plus 70 years." Some works by authors such as James Joyce, Rudyard Kipling, and A.E. Housman have regained copyright protection. (Although the copyright extension legislation in the U.S. only applied to works in copyright, in England works came out of the public domain.)

© On January 1, 1996, as a result of the General Agreement on Tariffs and Trade (commonly known as the GATT Treaty), certain foreign works that had lost copyright status in the United States were brought out of the public domain. A list of those works can be found in the *Federal Register,* beginning May 1, 1996, and subsequently every four months thereafter. They can also be found on the U.S. Copyright Office's Web site (*lcweb.loc.gov/copyright*).

Fair use

If you had to get permission every time you wanted to use a few words from a book in a term paper or needed to make a single copy of an article to read once you left the library or sang a few bars of "Blowin' in the Wind" while you drove down Highway 61, life would be a drag. Because such a tight (and ridiculous) hold on intellectual property would stifle learning and creativity, the copyright law does have limits to the exclusive rights of a copyright holder.

Section 107 of Title 17 states that the fair use of a copyrighted work, including using copyrighted material for purposes such as criticism, comment, news reporting, teaching (including multiple copies for classroom use), scholarship, or research, is not a copyright infringement.

This does *not* mean that all educational, research, or news reporting uses are fair. Section 107 states that at least four factors must be considered in determining whether a use is a fair use:

1. The *purpose and character* of the use, including whether such use is of a commercial nature or is for nonprofit or education purposes.
2. The *nature* of the work.
3. The *amount and substantiality* of the portion used in relation to the work as a whole.

4.   The *effect of the use* upon the potential market for or value of the work.

The key to determining fair use is the word "fair." Would the author of a copyrighted work think that the way in which you intend to use his or her material is fair?

Consider the following situations:

©   A fashion designer wants to use short phrases from works of Gertrude Stein on tags for a line of Zen clothing. The amount of the material is small, but the *purpose and character* of the use is for commercial gain. Would Gertrude Stein want her work to benefit a clothing manufacturer or designer?

©   A writer wants to include some passages from private letters of John Lennon in an article she is writing for *Rolling Stone*. Although the passages are brief, the letters by *nature* are private. It would not seem fair to the estate of John Lennon to use the material without permission.

©   It is often thought that any amount less than 250 words is fair use. What about 55 words? Did you know that 55 words represents one-half of Robert Frost's poem, "Stopping by Woods on a Snowy Evening?" This small *amount* of words is a *substantial* portion of Robert Frost's work.

©   A professor wants his students to read "A Clean, Well-Lighted Place" by Ernest Hemingway. He asks the students to copy the story out of an anthology in the library. The professor may argue that the copying would be for educational purposes, but Hemingway's publisher, Charles Scribner's Sons, could certainly cite a loss of royalty income from the lost sales as an *effect* the copying had on its property.

Any time you adapt copyrighted material without permission you're taking a risk. The copyright law and doctrine of fair use are written in broad language and are open to interpretation. The only true determination of fair use would be decided in a court of law. Give careful consideration before claiming fair use. When in doubt, ask for permission.

International law

This book discusses the United States copyright law and its ramifications for copyrighted works published or created in the United States. As the walls of our global village come down, it is even more apparent that we need to be familiar with international copyright law. With the click of a mouse we can distribute copyrighted material around the world and, conversely, we can print copyrighted material from around the world.

There is no common copyright law in the world. Countries have their own laws. By way of international treaties, countries have agreed to give each other the same copyright protection they give to their own country. The two major treaties are the Berne Convention for the Protection of Literary and Artistic Works and the Universal Copyright Convention. The United States joined the Berne Convention on March 1, 1989, and has been a member of the UCC since September 16, 1955.

If you are planning to distribute your copyrighted works outside of the United States, you will need to know the copyright law of the countries in which you will be distributing. One good resource for more information on the treaties and international law is *The Copyright Handbook, Fourth Edition* by attorney Stephen Fishman. (See Appendix A.)

Moral rights

Copyright law in many European and other countries grants additional rights to authors. These rights are known as moral rights or *droits morals.* Moral rights are different from the economic rights granted in U.S. law in that they do not terminate and cannot be transferred, even if copyright has been transferred. They are the artists' rights in perpetuity and pass on to the heirs. What are these moral rights?

© The right to prevent modification, distortion, or mutilation of the work in a way that would harm the artist's reputation or honor.

© The right of the artist to insist that his or her name be affixed on the work or *not* placed on works that are not theirs.

© The right of the artist to determine all aspects of public presentation of the work.

© The right of the artist to withdraw or disavow any work if it is changed or no longer represents the artist's idea.

Summary

Whether you are creating original works that you want to protect or are using the copyrighted works of others, it's important to understand the basics of copyright law.

There are two U.S. copyright laws you need to be familiar with. One governs works published before 1978; the other governs works created after 1978.

Highlights of the old law

© Publication was the key to protection.

© A term of copyright was 28 years with a 47-year renewal, for a total term of 75 years.

© The renewal term was extended to 67 years for works in copyright on October 27, 1998.

© Works must have displayed a valid copyright notice to be protected.

© A copyright had to be registered to be protected.

Highlights of the new law

© Creation in fixed form is the key to protection.

© A single term of copyright is defined as the life of the author plus 70 years for individuals, or 95 years from publication or 120 years from creation (whichever is first) for a company.

© A notice of copyright is optional after March 1, 1989 (although strongly recommended).

© Registration of copyright is optional (although strongly recommended).

© In 1992, copyright law was amended to include automatic renewal.

© Works are registered with the U.S. Copyright Office. If you have registration questions, you may call the office in Washington, D.C.

© The Copyright Office records are available to the public. To check on the copyright status of a work, you may search the records yourself, have the Copyright Office perform the search, or hire an independent search firm.

© A notice of copyright is advisable to let others know who owns the copyright to a given work.

©©©

© Knowing what material is in the public domain can be tricky. When in doubt have a copyright search performed.

© There are four factors of fair use: purpose and character; nature of the work copied (or used); amount and substantiality taken; and effect of the use on the market for the original work.

© Fair use is sometimes an overused concept. Don't claim fair use lightly. When in doubt, request permission to use copyrighted material or consult a copyright professional.

Chapter 4

Fair Use Examined

Perhaps the most frequently asked copyright question is: What is fair use? It seems as though most people understand that the property belongs to someone else; they just want to know how much they can use before they have broken the rules.

The four factors of fair use

A case of copyright infringement has been filed. The parties involved in the suit must bring their sides of the case to the court. The defense has claimed that the use of the copyrighted material was a fair use. The court will view the case through the paradigm of the four factors of fair use:

1. What are the *purpose and character* of the defendant's use?
2. What is the *nature* of the use?
3. How *much* of the plaintiff's material is used, and how *substantial* is the use?
4. Does the use have an *effect on the existing or potential market* of the plaintiff's material?

Barney vs. The San Diego Chicken

"I love you. You love me..." is how the world's most famous dinosaur, Barney, begins his famous song. Although the character is adored by young children, Barney often brings out the savage beast in those who are beyond the age of 7. The Internet is loaded with Barney-slamming Web sites. On the Web, the child-idol can be known as "Tyrannosaurus Wretch" or "The Purple Terror."

Lyons Partnership, Barney's owners, has traditionally chosen to ignore those who malign its character online. However, Lyons was not so loving when it came to the antics of the famed San Diego Chicken. In November 1997, Barney's owners filed a copyright infringement suit against Ted Giannoulas, the man inside the chicken costume.

As a part of his act, Giannoulas, dressed as the Chicken, would "punch, flip, stand on and otherwise assault the putative 'Barney.'" Giannoulas had been warned in 1994 that his Barney-banging act constituted copyright infringement, but the warning was ignored. At the time the suit was filed, Lyons' attorney stated that Giannoulas' use of the Barney character had caused "irreparable injury...[to] the distinctive quality of the Barney trademark."

Giannoulas' claimed that his use of the character in his act is a parody and therefore constituted a "fair use," which was protected under the Copyright Act. Lyons disagreed and sought damages of $100,000 for each time the dinosaur was used in the Chicken's routine. Commenting on the suit, Giannoulas said, "I used to think that Barney was a lovable character, but now I think he's just the biggest bully on the block. There have been plenty of parodies of Barney. They probably think that the Chicken is easy picking."

Barney vs. The San Diego Chicken, cont.

After tasting chicken-blood, Barney's owners went on a legal rampage, filing 70 infringement suits against shops, distributors, and performers for misuse of the Barney likeness.

Let's take a look at a few scenarios in which fair use is a key player.

A word from President Gerald Ford

A common misconception is that it is the number of words you want to use that determines fair use. "It's only 300 words, so it must be fair use. It's such a small amount." When determining fair use, you must consider all four of the factors.

In 1985, the Supreme Court ruled that the use of even a small amount of words from a substantial work was *not* a fair use. *The Nation* magazine had used about 300 words from former president Gerald Ford's 200,000-word memoirs in a story about Ford's decision to pardon former president Richard Nixon. Harper & Row (publisher of the memoirs) sued *The Nation* for infringing its copyright. Although *The Nation* argued that it was merely reporting the news (a favored use under the Section 107 fair-use test), Harper & Row argued that the use of the material in the article had a significant effect on the market of its property.

Time magazine had contracted with Harper & Row for a fee of $25,000 to run the "Nixon pardon" material. After an article ran in *The Nation, Time* canceled its contract and refused to pay the balance owed of $12,500. In a 6-to-3 decision, the Supreme Court held that *The Nation* had indeed violated copyright and that a fair-use defense did not apply.

Are databases copyright-protected?

A healthcare provider network has developed a database containing a variety of information including drug interaction information. Some of this data is published in the network's quarterly newsletter. Another network extracted this information from the newsletter and added it to its database of information. Is this use fair?

Prior to a landmark Supreme Court ruling, the "sweat-of-the-brow" determination in fact-gathering would probably have helped determine the outcome. On March 27, 1991, however, the U.S. Supreme Court decided unanimously that Feist Publications, a Kansas-based publisher of directories, did not infringe on the Rural Telephone Service when Feist copied the Telephone Service's white pages.

Justice Sandra Day O'Connor, writing for the Court, said, "The only conceivable expression is the manner in which the compiler has selected and arranged the facts. Thus, if the selection and arrangement are original, these elements of the work are eligible for copyright protection. No matter how original this format, however, the facts themselves do not become original through association."

The key consideration when determining the copyrightability of a database is original authorship—*how* the facts are selected and arranged. An alphabetical listing of all persons residing in a city, such as that published by Rural Telephone Service, does not exhibit any original authorship. Yet, if you select from that list all residents who subscribe to *The New Yorker* magazine and are older than 35 you may have added authorship to the database you have created.

What is a database?

An automated database is a body of facts, data, or other information assembled into an organized format suitable for use in a computer and comprising one or more files.

The copyright law does not specifically enumerate databases as copyright-protected, but legislative history indicates that Congress considers computer databases and compilations of data as "literary works" subject to copyright protection. Databases may be considered copyrightable as a form of compilation, which is defined in the law as a work "formed by the collection and assembling of pre-existing materials or of data that are selected, coordinated, or arranged in such a way that the resulting work as a whole constitutes an original work of authorship."

Source: Circular 65, "Copyright Registration for Automated Databases," U.S. Copyright Office.

Parody and fair use

A parody, according to *Webster's New World Dictionary*, is a "literary or musical work imitating the characteristic style of some other work or of a writer or composer in a satirical or humorous way, most typically by applying it to an inappropriate subject."

From Tom Stoppard's spin on Shakespeare (*Rosencrantz and Guildenstern are Dead*), to Anthony Hecht turning Matthew Arnold's poem *Dover Beach* into *Dover Bitch*, to Weird Al Yankovic's *Eat It,* a derivative work of Michael Jackson's *Beat It* (let it be known that Weird Al does get permission to make his adaptations), parodies have provided social commentary, criticism, and entertainment throughout history.

Parodies can serve the function of keeping certain artists or works from seeming too important. For example, although *American Gothic* has remained Grant Wood's creation, it is difficult to view the painting and not think of the myriad of parodies that have been created based on the painting.

The legal loophole utilized by parodists is the doctrine of fair use. Although parody is not directly mentioned in the Copyright Act, scholarship and commentary are both allowable exceptions to the law.

The guidelines used to identify whether a work can be seen as a parody and receive protection under the fair use provision of the Copyright Act include the following:

© The work may contain only enough of the original work to make it identifiable as a parody.

© The parody must create a new work that can stand on its own, while criticizing the original work.

What if the new work is in bad taste and its existence may hinder the sales of the original work? Although a parody's effect on the market for the original work is weighed when cases are heard, the Supreme Court maintains that if a work is identified as a parody, it will have a different market than the original work and should not hinder sales.

Therefore, Anthony Hecht was within his rights when he turned Matthew Arnold's love interest in *Dover Beach* into a prostitute in his parody *Dover Bitch: A Criticism of Life*.

Parody as an art form came under a great deal of scrutiny in the 1990s. The most celebrated suit was *Campbell v. Acuff-Rose*, or as it was better known, the case of *Pretty Woman*.

One of the central issues examined in the case was the definition of a derivative work. After refusing the rap group permission to record the song, Acuff-Rose filed an infringement suit, claiming that the group's version of the song was an unauthorized derivative of the original work. The group claimed that its song was a parody and, therefore, it represented a fair use of copyrighted material.

After four years in various courts, the Supreme Court upheld an artist's right to parody original works under existing fair use doctrine. Justice David Souter referred to the work as "transformative." Transformative-ness has become part of the fair-use test. It is different from a derivative work; the right to create derivative works belongs to the copyright owner. The more transformative the second work is, the more likely it will be considered fair use.

Although the Supreme Court upheld the right to comment or criticize original works through the creation of parodies, simply calling a work a parody does not guarantee protection against an infringement suit. The courts will continue to have the final say on whether a use is fair.

The latter half of the 1990s saw several trivia books brought before the courts in copyright infringement suits. *The Seinfeld Aptitude Test* contained 600 multiple choice questions based on dialogue, characters, plot elements, and locations from the popular TV series *Seinfeld.* The creator of the book, Carol Publishing Group, claimed that the book contained only "facts" about the series and that these "facts" were not protected by copyright. However, the court rejected the defense, finding that the publisher had failed to prove protection under three of the four factors of fair use. The publisher appealed the decision, but it was upheld in a Court of Appeals the following year. The judge found that the book did not quiz true facts, such as the identity of the actors or the time it takes to shoot an episode, but rather "facts" that were really elements of the show that *were* protected by copyright. Carol Publishing Group was in court again later in the year for a similar suit involving a *Star Trek* trivia book it had produced.

A word of caution: Fair use is about risk. How much risk are you willing to take? How much time and money are you willing to expend to defend your risk? Would it be worth the trouble? Wouldn't it be better to spend a few dollars for permission rather than countless dollars in court?

You've reviewed your use through the four factors and are still not sure if your use is a fair use. If you have any doubt, it may be wise to paraphrase or request permission.

Summary

One of the most misunderstood (and overused) concepts in copyright law is that of fair use. Here are some of the keys to remember:

©   Section 107 of the copyright law identifies four factors that must be considered when claiming a fair use of copyrighted material: the *purpose* and *character* of the use; the *nature* of the use; the *amount* and *substantiality* of the use; and the *effect* of the use on the market for the original work.

©   The Gerald Ford case proved that even a very small amount (300 words of a 200,000-word manuscript) may not be considered fair use.

©   A collection of factual information alone is not copyrightable. However, if the collection of data has authorship, or originality, then it is protected by copyright.

©   Parody (the criticism or satirization of another's work) is protected as freedom of speech. However, simply claiming a work is a parody does not automatically protect it against a copyright infringement suit.

©   When you claim fair use, you take a risk. The wording of fair use language in the Copyright Act is vague and subject to interpretation by the courts.

Chapter 5

The Printed Word

When Johann Gutenberg invented the printing press in 1456, little did he realize that he was setting more than type in motion. Look around. Print is everywhere, from books to magazines, from food labels to footwear! Clearly, the definition of "the printed word" encompasses much more than Gutenberg's Bible and other books mass produced from a printing press. In turn, the protection afforded by copyright law covers much more than books and magazines.

As we discussed earlier, under the current copyright laws in the United States, words are copyrighted as soon as they are put in "fixed form." In addition to the books, magazines, and newspapers you buy at the bookstore, this might include a letter to your aunt, a poem from your sweetheart, your first grader's story about her pet turtle, your son's dissertation, your accounting firm's marketing brochure, or your prepared acceptance speech for your Nobel prize.

Again, it's the *expression* of the ideas that is copyrightable, not the idea or the fact itself. In other words, if you have an idea for a story, a play, a poem, or a screenplay, and you don't write it down in some way, no matter how much you have developed it in your head, it's not protected by copyright.

Book publishing

Copyright is a key issue for anyone involved in book publishing, but particularly for the writer, the creator of the intellectual property. Why? *Revenue.* For each book sold, the writer receives payment. If the work is copied, sold, or used in some way without the knowledge or permission of the writer, he or she loses the opportunity to profit from the work.

The National Writers Union expressed its concern about the dangers of copyright infringement by describing "the decline in the standard of living of most writers, as well as of other creators—a decline due in large part to the stagnation, or outright decline, in pay; the theft of our work by large media corporations [that] commercially exploit our work and pocket the profit; and the seizure of an ever broader spectrum of rights by publishers who pay the same or less money than was paid for print publication rights."

Trade books vs. textbooks

An important distinction needs to be made between trade books (those books published to be marketed to the general public, usually through bookstores) and textbooks (those books published primarily to be used in an educational setting).

With many trade books, the copyright remains with the author. The publisher buys the publishing rights, which means that for a period of time, as specified in the author's contract, the publisher has the right to control how and when the work is published. This may include the right to grant reprint permission when another author wants to excerpt or adapt the material in another book. (Although it is not the norm, some authors reserve the right to review all requests to have their material reprinted.) When a book goes out of print, the rights generally revert to the author.

In terms of copyright, textbooks are viewed differently. Most trade books are generated by the author's idea. Textbooks are generally initiated by a publisher. Acquisitions editors employed by publishers work with teachers and professors to determine what types of books are needed in classrooms. The editor then finds the appropriate author and contracts with him or her to write the book. Copyright generally stays with the publisher.

Subsidiary rights

Even though the primary product in book publishing is the book, copyright protection isn't limited to the book itself. Print rights are often only the starting point for a literary property. If a book sells well, it may prove marketable in other forms. For example, a popular fiction book may become a movie, an audio tape, or even a play. A nonfiction book that sells well may become an audio tape, a computer program, a training video, or a multimedia CD-ROM.

The rights to negotiate separately for audio, software, foreign translation, or other rights are generally described in an author's book contract. The author or agent and the publisher clarify which parties have the right to negotiate the rights for future products based on the original book. In rare cases, the subsidiary rights can even be sold before the book is written. A savvy author will understand what rights are negotiable and how the revenue will be divided between author and publisher.

Anthologies and collections

What about a book featuring the writings of several individuals? Does the publisher of an anthology or other collection of works hold the copyright? Typically, the publisher holds *no* rights to selections in an anthology.

For example, an anthology of English literature may contain works by a variety of authors, essayists, and poets. Some of the material may be in the public domain (such as works published in the 19th century) and some may be protected by copyright. Those copyright-protected works generally appear "by permission" of the copyright holder. Unless the publisher happens to be the copyright holder for some of the selections in the anthology, it holds no rights for the selections.

What *does* the publisher hold the rights to? The anthology publisher does control some of what goes into an anthology:

©   The process of compilation, or the way the works are selected and compiled in the anthology.

©   Cover art and any art created to accompany the text.

©   The foreword, preface, chapter introductions, and any other material newly created for the anthology.

Anthology publishers are often bombarded with requests to reprint material to which they hold no rights. Typically they respond to such requests by referring the requester to the copyright holder—the owner of the underlying work. Often, they will simply send a letter referencing the request, followed by a box checked next to the sentence, "Not our material."

If you wish to reprint or use some material that appears in an anthology, you can often find the source of the material on the copyright page of the anthology. Here, the publisher may list the copyright information regarding the reprinted material appearing in the book. If there is no information here, you might check the acknowledgment page. Often, the publisher or the editor of the compilation will acknowledge the contributors to the work. If this doesn't offer any clues, you may then be forced to rely on the publisher to provide you with the information.

Tables, charts, and graphs

Many books, particularly nonfiction works, include graphic components—tables of information, pie charts, elaborate graphs, and so forth—that others may want to reprint or use.

Often, the publisher does not own the copyright for these components. They may have been reprinted from other sources or provided by experts. Often, the publisher acknowledges the source with a credit line on the copyright page or, possibly, in the acknowledgments.

Letters

Where F. Scott Fitzgerald once wooed Zelda with pen and paper, today's young lovers bill and coo via computer. Parents no longer need to check the mailbox for letters from their dorm-bound college students—they need only check their e-mail.

Regardless of how often they write letters, most people do not think of their everyday correspondences as having great literary value. But they may be surprised to learn that copyright law has always protected personal letters as a form of intellectual property.

The general rule regarding personal correspondence is that the author of a letter retains the ownership of the copyright, the literary property, and the recipient of the letter acquires ownership of the physical property (the paper and ink). The author has the exclusive right to permit or prevent the copying of the letter and its publication. The recipient has the right to destroy or preserve the letter, show it to others, deposit it in a library, or transfer possession of the physical property. This rule applies whether the author is Bill Gates writing a letter to the editor of *Newsweek* in response to an article about Microsoft or a man writing a letter to his brother to offer advice on growing prize-winning tomatoes.

Even though copyright remains with the author, the time at which a letter was written is important in determining how reprint permission should be handled. Letters written before January 1, 1978 (the date the current copyright law was enacted) are protected under common law. As is the case today, the copyright for a letter is held by the author. However, the factor determining who holds the copyright is publication.

If the letter was never published (as is the case with most letters), the copyright stays in perpetuity with the author and his or her heirs. However, if the letter was published, the author can hold the copyright for a term of up to 95 years, after which the letter is in the public domain.

Publication is not a factor in determining the term of copyright for letters written *after* January 1, 1978. Under the current law, letters are protected by copyright from the moment they are fixed in a tangible means of expression, such as on paper, regardless of whether they are ever published. Existing copyright law sets the term of copyright on letters as the life of the author plus 70 years.

However, under a special provision of the copyright law, works of original authorship that were unpublished as of January 1, 1978 are protected by copyright until at least December 31, 2002. (If the work remains unpublished as of December 31, 2002, copyright will expire 70 years after the author's death. If the author died before January 1, 1953, copyright expires on December 31, 2002.) This means that if a person wishes to use an unpublished letter that was written prior to January 1, 1978, he or she must obtain permission from the author or the author's heirs at least until the end of the term of protection in 2002, but possibly longer.

This is of particular importance to historians, biographers, and other scholars. Consider the following real-life example: An educational textbook publisher wanted to include a letter written by George Washington in a history textbook. The letter was part of the George Washington Papers in the Manuscript Division of the Library of Congress. The publisher's permissions manager wrote for permission to reprint the letter in the text. She was informed that they could neither grant nor deny permission. The writer of the letter, under common law, had the sole right to publish the property, and that right had descended to his heirs. Finding the heirs of George Washington could prove difficult. Without their permission, publishing the letter would definitely be taking a risk.

In this case, the publisher decided that the letter was important enough to the book that it was worth the risk. If the heirs came forward, the publisher was prepared to take responsibility for including the letter without permission.

Scholarly writings

"Publish or perish" is a familiar philosophy in the academic community. In order to maintain your professional reputation, it is essential to write—either books or articles for professional journals. Otherwise, you won't be as strong a candidate for tenure, department chair, etc.

As experts in their respective fields, college and university professors represent the cutting edge of research and thought, and they offer the basis for further research by students and others. It is through their writings that new theories get proposed, debated, proven, or debunked. Medical journals such as the *Journal of the American Medical Association* are often looked to by the medical community as well as by the media for the latest information on the diagnosis and treatment of disease and illness.

A professor's work moves from a doctoral thesis to a scholarly book with a limited printing to a college textbook with a large audience. So, too, moves the value of the work from a pure academic work to a more commercial property. A professor may want to incorporate other copyrighted materials into his or her work. He or she will have to receive permission to use the other work or pay royalties if using the other work is not a fair use. Although the professor may have been able to claim academic fair use in his or her thesis, the textbook being sold to 30,000 students creates a different situation.

Newspapers

The focus of most newspapers is to report facts—and facts are not copyright-protected. The first newspaper that reports the story of an airplane crash, for example, does not own the copyright to the facts. Anyone may read the facts from the newspaper and then write his or her own story. He or she doesn't even have to cite the paper as the source of the facts. However, the way in which the facts are presented is protected by copyright.

In fact, many newspapers do well because of the way they describe the facts of a given situation. *The New York Times* and *The Wall Street Journal* are popular because they are considered sources of highly reliable and well-written information. But whether it is a major exposé, a feature on fashions, a comic strip, or a weather report, these tangible forms of expression are copyrighted.

The copyright to these works may not be held by the newspaper in which they appear. Newspapers use a combination of staff, freelance, and syndicated writers, artists, and photographers. A close look at the material in question can give clues as to the copyright owner. Does the byline say staff writer? Associated Press? Or Copyright 1997 King Features?

Magazines

Most periodicals have staff writers who contribute to the publication, but nonetheless many articles are written by freelance writers (as are some newspaper articles.) When a freelance writer sells a piece to a magazine for publication, he or she is often selling the "First North American Serial Rights." This means that the magazine is purchasing the rights to publish the piece for the first time in North America. The author generally retains the copyright to the article.

The rights are also considered "nonexclusive," which means that the author/copyright holder is free to sell the right to publish the piece in other publications, or perhaps in a book he or she compiles. The rights holder is also able to grant permission to others who wish to publish, excerpt, or adapt the work in another publication, such as a textbook, anthology, or other collection. (Once again, know who holds the rights before you request reprint permission.)

Work for hire

Who owns the copyright to a contributed work? This can be confusing. Is it a work for hire or does the author own the rights? If the author is an employee of the company publishing the work—be it a magazine, feature, news story, corporate newsletter, or marketing brochure—and the work is done as part of the employee's duties on the job, the copyright belongs to the employer. However, if the author is not an employee of the company publishing the work—if he or she works as an independent contractor hired only for specific projects—the copyright issue may not be as clear. Consider the following examples:

Example 1: A woman is employed as a copywriter in the marketing department of a large corporation. Her job responsibilities include writing articles for the company newsletter. She writes an article about the company's wellness program for the newsletter. The article is well-written and well-received throughout the company. The author decides that the piece would fit well in the corporate news section of the city's major newspaper. Can she submit the article to the newspaper for publication?

Most likely the *company* owns the copyright to the piece because it pays the woman's salary and she wrote the article as part of her job. The company may be thrilled to have such a positive article about its commitment to employee health published in the paper. But as copyright holder, the employer must give permission before the work can be published.

Example 2: Let's look at the same copywriter in a slightly different situation. She still works for the same corporation in the same capacity. However, she also does freelance writing on the side. Inspired by the research she did for the piece on her company's corporate wellness program, she decides to write an article on smoking-cessation programs. She researches and writes the article during evenings and weekends. She writes her article and submits it for publication to the same major newspaper. The piece is published and she is paid the standard fee for pieces similar in length to hers. She owns the copyright to the piece for this and future publications.

Example 3: Our copywriter has left her full-time job to pursue freelance writing as a career. She is hired by her former employer to write another piece for the same newsletter she used to work on. She negotiates the right to retain copyright on the piece. The company pays her slightly less for the piece, but she maintains ownership as well as the right to sell the piece again.

Electronic communication and freelancers

The growth of the Internet has added a new dimension to freelance writing—as well as a great deal of tension between freelance writers and the publications to whom they sell their work. For example, many newspapers have started online versions of their papers. They work with a particular service or post their articles with an online database. The articles are then available for reading, printing, or downloading by online service members or Internet users, sometimes for a fee.

So what's the problem? Don't freelance writers want their material distributed electronically? That's generally not the issue. The freelance writers sold only "First North American Rights" to the publication. The companies have allowed the work to be made available through the most easily accessible (and least restricted) means of transmitting information in the history of the world. And the writers, the copyright holders, *aren't getting paid*. The writers contend that they never sold the electronic rights to their work and that publishers are committing copyright infringement by posting their work without permission.

Tasini v. The New York Times

In 1997, a Manhattan judge ruled that a group of publishers was within its rights to include its publications in online databases without the permission (and without further compensation) of the freelance writers whose work made up much of the publications. The landmark case, *Tasini v.* The New York Times, dealt a major blow to the writers, who believed that they had not sold their work for electronic distribution.

The decision was overturned in the U.S. Court of Appeals for the Second Circuit in late 1999 when the court found that the writers (represented by Jonathan Tasini, president of the National Writers Union) had their copyrights infringed upon when their articles were republished online and on CD-ROMs.

This decision represents a major victory for freelance writers, and it underscores the importance of clearly worded contracts between those who create intellectual properties and those who use and distribute them.

Protecting freelance writers

As the debate between writers and publishers continues, two organizations have joined forces to protect the interests of freelance writers. Early in 1996, the National Writers Union and the UnCover Company announced a partnership that will allow writers to receive royalties for articles ordered through the UnCover system.

UnCover represents one of the world's largest databases of magazine and journal articles, claiming 7 million citations from 17,000 periodicals. In order to handle the royalties generated by the new venture, the NWU created the Publication Rights Clearinghouse.

This clearinghouse was formed primarily to support writers by helping them get paid for the use of their work. The UnCover system is the creation of the CARL Corporation, a for-profit organization developed out of the Colorado Alliance of Research Libraries. Both UnCover and CARL are wholly owned affiliates of Knight-Ridder Information, Inc.

In a March 1996 press release, Rebecca T. Lenzini, president of CARL Corporation, stated, "We have always been diligent about copyright fees. This exciting arrangement with the National Writers Union uses existing technology to make sure creators receive a fair share of the revenue from the emerging information industry. We are pleased to have the NWU as a partner in our mission of making journal and magazine material available both quickly and economically throughout the world, while affirming the principles of copyright."

NWU President Jonathan Tasini added, "We look forward to turning this model of copyright clearance into the standard of the electronic database industry. Publication Rights Clearinghouse also expects to share and develop collective-licensing solutions with other companies in the business of reusing the works of freelancers—whether via full-text databases, CD-ROMs or the World Wide Web."

UnCover is a searchable periodical database and delivery service. Articles can be delivered via fax in 24 hours or less. The UnCover Reveal Alert service is also available, which automatically sends the tables of contents from specific periodicals directly to a subscriber's e-mail box on a weekly basis.

Users search the database for free, but incur costs when articles are downloaded. The base rate (not including copyright fees) is $8.50 for articles ordered directly by users and $10 for articles ordered through the UnCover staff. Payment is made by major credit cards or through other billing or payment options. (See Appendix for contact information on the NWU and UnCover.)

Summary

The ability to copy and distribute the printed word has changed dramatically since the invention of the printing press. Words are now copyrighted as soon as they are in a fixed form. Regardless of what form of the printed word you are working with, here are some key ideas to keep in mind:

- © The risk of infringement increases as the potential profit increases.
- © Copyright holders must be diligent about protecting the rights to their words, because their words are their property, and property has value.
- © Rights to the printed word don't end with publication or serial rights. A book may become an audio or video tape, a movie, a play, or a CD-ROM.
- © Don't assume that the copyright holder for a particular work is the same as the publisher of the book (or periodical) in which the work appears.
- © Letters are protected by copyright just as any other intellectual property is.
- © The key to the term of copyright of a letter is when it was written—before or after 1978.
- © Freelance writers typically sell First North American Serial Rights, which allows the periodical that purchases those rights to publish the work one time in its publication.
- © Copyright ownership in contributed works can be confusing. Understand your written agreement clearly before signing.
- © The marketplace for freelance magazine and newspaper articles is changing greatly with the advent of electronic delivery of information.

Chapter 6

Visual Arts

W ho owns the rights to Grant Wood's *American Gothic*? What rights are involved in creating reproductions or photographs of the painting? And who owns the rights to the newly created work? What about advertisements? Are they protected by copyright? Who owns the rights to family photos taken at a studio? They're of your family, so you should own the copyright on the photos, right? All of these issues fall within the realm of copyright protection of visual arts.

Defining works of visual art for copyright purposes can be a bit tricky. For example, some visual images are protected by copyright but are not defined as a work of visual art.

Copyright law defines visual art as:

©   A still photographic image produced for exhibition purposes only, existing in a single copy that is signed by the author, or in a limited edition of 200 copies or fewer that are signed and consecutively numbered by the author.

©   A painting, drawing, print, or sculpture, existing in a single copy, in a limited edition of 200 or fewer copies that are signed and consecutively numbered by the author, or, in the case of a sculpture, in multiple cast, carved, or fabricated sculptures of 200 or fewer that are consecutively numbered by the author and bear the signature of other identifying mark of the author.

A work of visual art does not include:

© Any poster, map, globe, chart, technical drawing, diagram, model, applied art, motion picture, or other audiovisual work, book, magazine, newspaper, periodical, database, electronic information service, electronic publication, or similar publication.

© Any merchandising item or packaging material.

© Any portion or part of any item described in the first two listings.

The Visual Artists Rights Act

For the first time, Congress accorded "moral rights" to creators of works of visual art with the Visual Artists Rights Act of 1990 (VARA). Although any original work committed to fixed form was already protected by copyright, VARA extended the rights of creators of visual art. Under VARA, the following acts are prohibited:

© Any intentional distortion, mutilation, or other modification of the work that would be prejudicial to the artist's honor or reputation.

© Destruction of a work of recognized stature.

© Use of the artist's name with a work that the author did not create.

© Use of the artist's name with a work that has been modified.

VARA was enacted shortly after the United States joined the Berne Copyright Convention (see Chapter 3), which acknowledges an author's rights of attribution and integrity. These rights cannot be transferred, nor do they ever expire.

Say an artist is hired to paint a large mural for a community airport. Several years after the work is completed, the artist gains worldwide fame. The airport that commissioned the mural decides that the people who pass through the facility might want to purchase items depicting the mural painted by the now-famous artist, so it orders coffee mugs, T-shirts, and coasters bearing a replica of the mural and the name of the airport. Someone sends the artist one of the items bearing his artwork. Based on his rights under VARA, the artist has the right to stop the airport from producing commercial items using his art.

Before VARA, the mural would have been treated solely as a property. The artist would have had no say in this matter. Now, the author can even remove his name from the work. Moral rights, however, can be waived. The waiver should be in writing.

The scope of works covered under VARA is quite narrow. It includes paintings, drawings, prints, sculptures, and limited edition photographs. Works must be produced in a "limited edition" of 200 copies or fewer, with each piece being numbered and signed by the artist.

The following types of art are specifically excluded: posters, motion pictures, audiovisual works, books, magazines, databases, electronic media, advertisements, packaging materials, and any work that is not copyrightable.

Reproductions

If you created a painting or sculpture today (outside of a work-for-hire arrangement), you would hold the copyright to the work. But what about classic works, such as the Mona Lisa? If they're in the public domain, that means you can do whatever you want with them, right? Well, yes and no.

It is true that the Mona Lisa is in the public domain, but the actual painting is part of a collection housed at the Louvre in Paris. Along with the right to charge admission to view the works they house, the museum can control the rights to reproduce the works or to license those rights to others. This is why many museums won't allow you to take pictures of the items in their collections.

If a work of fine art is protected by copyright, the copyright holder maintains (or can transfer) all the rights accorded to any copyright holder, including the right to reproduce and distribute the work. Therefore, before creating and marketing a necktie that features Dali's *Persistence of Memory,* find out who holds the copyright and ask for permission.

Photography

When Mathew Brady captured his famous Civil War images, little did he know what impact the medium would have on copyright and its issues. Whether it's a limited-edition Robert Mapplethorpe shot on display, an award-winning newspaper photo, or a family portrait taken in a studio, photographs are set in fixed form and are covered by copyright. Limited-edition photography are accorded additional protection under VARA.

Freelance/work-for-hire photography

Photographers generally hold the copyright on their work. If photos are taken while a photographer is working as an employee of a company, the copyright generally belongs to the employer.

Freelance photographers share many of the challenges of freelance writers (see Chapter 5). As with freelance writing assignments, concerns over who holds what rights can be avoided by the creation of a written agreement that outlines the rights of all parties at the outset of the job.

Many publishers go to great lengths (beyond the creation of a written agreement) to retain the copyright to photographs taken on their behalf, particularly with independent photographers. To fully establish their claim, some companies will provide photographic equipment and supplies and reimburse the photographer for mileage to and from the site.

Photography and the electronic age

The rapid growth of digital technology has made it increasingly easy for photographers to create, store, market, and distribute their works. Once an image is "digitized" (saved in digital format), it can be stored in a database for easy Internet viewing, copied onto a disk or CD for shipment, or even sent to a client via e-mail as a file attachment.

But along with these benefits come new concerns. Once an image is put in digital form, it can be easily copied and transferred—with or without permission of the copyright holder. Images can also be easily altered using a variety of software programs—again, with or without permission. Other concerns arise when photographers contract with large photo licensing agencies, which often require long-term contracts (sometimes as long as 20 years). In addition, a photo can easily be transmitted to a client without the inclusion of the proper photo credit, which is often the only way anyone could know to whom the photo belongs.

For more information on photo copyright, consult *The Law (In Plain English) for Photographers* by Leonard D. DuBoff (see Appendix A).

Studio photography

The effects of technology have even reached local photo shops, many of which now feature "digital imaging" machines that allow users not only to duplicate any photo they bring in, but to alter the photo, including removing unwanted people. If a person gets divorced, for example, but wants to preserve his or her own image in the wedding photos, he or she can go to the photo shop and have the ex-spouse cropped out. However—consumer beware—this may be copyright infringement.

How can I commit copyright infringement with my own wedding photos? They're mine, people think. Consider the following scenario: You find a stack of photos showing family members from the World War I era. The photos are slightly cracked and faded, but you can still identify Old Uncle Henry and the tattooed lady the family legend says he dated. You've heard about a local photo shop that advertises a "digital imaging" machine that will not only reproduce the photos, but will restore them to their original quality.

You are told that the store will not reproduce the photos for you because the backs of the pictures are stamped with the name of the studio that took the photos. You must obtain reprint permission from the studio, which holds the copyright to the photos. You explain that the studio certainly went out of business many, many years ago. The photo shop manager suggests that you try to find the heirs of the studio owners.

You are clearly not making a profit by cleaning up an old family photo (as opposed to scanning the photo for a book that will be sold to the public), but the photo is protected by copyright because it is in fixed form. The exclusive rights of a copyright holder include the right to alter or reproduce the work. The right to alter the photo or make copies remains with the copyright holder. In this example, it's the studio.

Keep in mind that most camera store owners are not this familiar with copyright law. Many stores attempt to comply with the law by posting a notice on the wall and near the imaging machines themselves that describes the rights held by copyright holders. Yet the stores are put in a difficult position. They must comply with the law while not making the process so cumbersome that their customers will lose interest in the benefits of the new technology.

In a related case involving a copy shop, a freelance designer was preparing a brochure for an upcoming conference.

He brought a photo of one of the conference speakers to the shop to have it scanned. The speaker himself had personally provided the photo. Unfortunately for the designer, the photo was stamped with the name of the studio that shot the photo. The copy shop would not reproduce the image without written permission from the studio.

Sculpture

A movie production company filming *Batman Forever* included some building shots in one scene. The film company got the required permits, including the permission of the building owners at the locations of the shoots. The right to film a building would include anything—including a sculpture—that happened to be on the property, right? Wrong.

The sculpture that caused the flap is titled *Zanja Madre* (meaning "Mother Ditch"), and was created by Minneapolis-based sculptor Andrew Leicester. The work appears in downtown Los Angeles, where part of *Batman Forever* was filmed.

Copyright law makes pieces of visual art, including sculpture, eligible for copyright protection. Warner Brothers was granted permission to film by the owner of the building in front of which the sculpture is located. However, the sculptor did not transfer his copyright to the building owner. Therefore, the right to film the sculpture was not necessarily included in the right to film the building.

Not only was the statue used in the film and the marketing materials, it was reproduced to scale for use in some of the film's scenes.

Cartoons and comic strips

Cartoons and comic strips have been a part of American life for almost as long as there have been newspapers. Characters such as Blondie, Snoopy, Garfield, and, more recently,

Dilbert are as well-known as our sports figures or political leaders. Syndicated cartoons appear in newspapers worldwide and are reproduced in books regularly. Greatly enhancing the revenue picture is product licensing based on favorite characters from popular strips. But how are reprint rights for cartoons handled?

As authors and artists continue to fight for greater control over the copyright of their works, so too are cartoonists engaged in an ongoing battle to hold on to what they create. The majority of major cartoon strips are controlled by syndicates, such as United Media (*Peanuts, Garfield*), King Features (*Blondie, Beetle Bailey, Hagar the Horrible*), and Universal Press (*Doonesbury*). It should also be noted that the major syndicates handle not only cartoonists, but syndicated columnists such as Mike Royko and Ann Landers. The copyright on most cartoons has been held by syndicates since William Randolph Hearst introduced the idea of syndication in the 1920s.

Syndicates have long been known for signing cartoonists to iron-clad, relatively one-sided contracts that leave artists with little or no control over their future work. Standard contracts give the syndicate all rights to the characters of a given strip, as well as the majority of the renewal options on the contract. In other words, a cartoonist who signs with a syndicate may no longer hold the rights to the characters he or she has created. If the artist is unhappy with the agreement, he or she is unable to take the strip elsewhere. If a cartoonist does leave a syndicate, the syndicate is often free to hire another artist to continue drawing the strip.

On the other hand, it would be a huge task for a struggling cartoonist to shop his work to the thousands of newspapers around the country. The syndicates provide an invaluable amount of exposure to cartoonists, and they handle the accounting for royalties and licensing agreements.

In recent years, a number of cartoonists have challenged the syndicates. The first came from Bill Keane, creator of

Charles Schulz' *Peanuts*

The creator of some of the world's best known intellectual properties, Charles Schulz died in February, 2000. His famous strip, which debuted in 1950, would eventually appear in more than 2,600 newspapers in 75 countries, be translated into 21 languages, and be read by 355 million people worldwide.

Although Schulz didn't own the copyright to the strip (it's controlled by United Media), he did maintain a certain level of control over how and where the characters could be used, including making sure that no one else would ever draw the strip. Schulz did authorize certain artists to create art for new merchandising and advertising ventures, but not to create new strips. However, the old strips will continue to rerun in newspapers around the world.

And although Schulz didn't own Charlie Brown, Lucy, Linus, Snoopy, and the other characters he created, he did realize royalties that exceeded $40 million dollars annually from merchandising agreements.

Family Circus. Ever since he successfully regained the copyright to his work after threatening to file a very public lawsuit, other cartoonists have begun waging their own battles.

Cartoonists who have taken legal action against their syndicate include Cathy Guisewite of *Cathy*, Lynn Johnston of *For Better or For Worse*, and Jim Unger of *Herman.* Unger won control of *Herman* and now operates his own firm, LaughingStock, which licenses reprints of *Herman.* Berke Breathed, creator of the popular strip *Bloom County,* won back control of his characters from the Washington Post Writers Group. He then retired the strip, assuring that the syndicate could not hire another cartoonist to draw his characters.

Licensing is a piece of the syndication picture that takes on great significance. With the decline in newspaper readership, some in the syndication business feel that the industry would not survive without licensing comic strip characters for other merchandise. Revenues from merchandise such as *Dilbert* calendars, Garfield toys that hang from car windshields, and *Peanuts* greeting cards, not to mention the rights to produce animated television shows and movies, can far outweigh the revenues that come from strip appearances in newspapers.

When requesting permission to reprint or use comic strips or characters from cartoons, the same rules apply as with other literary works. First, you must identify the copyright holder. The paper in which a comic appears is rarely the party that grants reprint permission. Most often, permission is granted by the syndicate that holds the rights. The name of the syndicate is generally printed between the frames of the strip, or somewhere along the border of a single frame cartoon. The next most important piece of information is the date the cartoon was printed in the paper. The date is generally drawn into the corner of one of the frames, along with the name of the artist(s) who drew the strip.

Some syndicates are developing a cross-referencing system to identify the captions and subject matter of strips. This will be particularly helpful if the requester needs reproducible art, as most syndicates are unable to identify a specific comic without the date it was printed. So if you want permission to use a particular *Peanuts* cartoon, you can probably get permission from United Media. But until a cross-referencing database is in wide use among cartoon syndicates, you may have a hard time getting reproducible art for your publication if all you know is the dialogue that appeared in the cartoon and you don't know the date the strip appeared.

Paintings and fine art

Before the Copyright Act of 1976, artists generally controlled reproduction rights to their original work, and a printer or other artist who copied the work controlled the rights to the copy or reproduction. This changed with the new law: The artist (or the artist's heirs) now retains the copyright for the original work *as well as* for copies or reproductions of the original work, unless the artist or heirs transfer those rights to someone else. In addition, all art works created after March 1, 1989 are protected by copyright, regardless of whether they have been registered with the Copyright Office.

Although the 1976 act helped to spell out artists' rights, the application of copyright to visual art remains a complicated matter. Works published prior to March 1, 1989 that were not previously registered may have fallen into the public domain in the United States. However, those works may still be protected by copyright outside of the United States, where copyright laws vary greatly from country to country. In fact, some works that were previously in the public domain outside the United States may have come out of the public domain to regain copyright protection. There is clearly cause for confusion over pre-1989 works and whether reprint permission is needed for reproductions.

A significant change in copyright law took effect on January 1, 1996, as a result of the General Agreement on Tariffs and Trade, commonly known as the GATT Treaty. This new legislation brought certain foreign works out of the public domain in the United States and has restored copyright protection. (See Chapter 3 for more details on the GATT Treaty.)

Print advertisements

Let's say you're publishing a marketing textbook and you want to use some ads that have appeared in magazines and newspapers. Companies create ads in order to promote and sell their products, so you're doing them a favor by giving them more exposure, right? You probably won't even need permission, but you decide to ask just as a formality. Why would any company object to having their ad used in a textbook?

It's not hard to make such assumptions. After all, companies spend millions upon millions of dollars to advertise their products each year. So you might be tempted to assume that they would jump at the chance to have their ad viewed by thousands of students. Some companies *will* jump at the chance.

However, more times than not, corporations will have some very specific questions they want answered, such as:

©   How is the ad being used?

©   Will the ad provide a negative example of anything?

©   Is the ad being used as an example of bad advertising?

©   What will the text say that surrounds the ad, and when can I see it?

And after they consider your request, some companies will refuse permission, for a variety of reasons. (As we will discuss in Chapter 11, copyright holders have the right to say no to permission requests.)

Although advertisers are eager to promote their products, they want to market them in a particular way, to a very specific segment of their market. Publishing an ad in your book might expose the product to an unwanted market segment. For example, a company that manufacturers alcoholic beverages may not want its products to be exposed to college students in a textbook. Another company might feel that you have interpreted its ad to convey a message that was not intended.

Another complication is the appearance of *people* in the ads. A company might grant permission for an ad that doesn't feature people, but the same company may not grant permission if models were used in creating the ad. In many cases, the company holds the rights to the ad itself, but the models who appeared in the ad have retained the rights to the use of their image. Although model releases can be obtained, they can be accompanied by a hefty fee.

Some things to keep in mind when considering reprinting a company's ad:

© Most companies diligently protect the copyright on their ads, as well as their trademarks and the way they are used and displayed.

© Be prepared to do some legwork in order to identify the copyright holder for a particular ad.

© The permission process for ads can be tricky and lengthy. Start with a company's public relations or marketing department, although you'll most likely be referred to the legal department or the corporate attorney.

© If you are requesting reproducible art along with permission to reprint the ad, allow extra time, and anticipate having to work with the company's ad agency.

© Look for the most current ads possible. You're less likely to be refused if the company considers the ad to be in keeping with its current public image.

© Be prepared to have the company offer you an alternate ad that is more current than the one you requested.

© Request additional ads from a variety of companies, because you may get refused for some of the ads you request.

Summary

Understanding copyright protection for visual arts can be challenging. The rights for different types of visual art are often handled in different ways, and held by different parties. Moral rights are now an important consideration in the copyright of visual art. Here are some important things to keep in mind regarding copyright and visual art:

©   The Visual Artists Rights Act (VARA) of 1990 spells out the copyright protection in relation to visual art.

©   A key component of VARA is that it protects "one-of-a-kind works" such as paintings, prints, photographs, drawings, and sculptures in single or limited (200 or less) editions.

©   VARA does not apply to a number of types of visual art, including promotional art, packaging, maps, posters, and technical drawings.

©   Fair use, or the allowable use without having to ask permission, rarely applies to works of fine art.

©   Regardless of how easy it may become to duplicate photographs, studios hold the rights to the photographs they have produced.

©   Photo archives are a tremendous resource for finding a wide variety of reproducible images for use in your publication.

©   When seeking permission for cartoons, identify the syndicate that holds the rights and get the date the strip was published.

©   Companies are particular about the ways in which their print ads are used. Request the most current ads possible, and request alternates in preparation for refusals.

Chapter 7

Performing Arts

T he very word "performing" seems contrary to copyright. The law states that in order to be copyrighted, a work must be in "fixed form." In order for "performance" to fall within the protection of copyright, the motion of the performing needs to be fixed—stationary—to be protected. For example, it is not Baryshnikov's leap across the stage that is copyright-protected, but rather the frame of film capturing the leap that fixes the motion of dance. How are other forms of the performing arts copyrighted?

Motion pictures

Motion pictures are protected by copyright as an audiovisual work. As with the multimedia presentations described in Chapter 9, motion pictures pose complex and sometimes confusing questions regarding copyright protection.

Most major motion pictures involve a screenplay, the film itself, and a soundtrack. If the screenplay is based on another work, such as a novel, a play, or a short story (as many are), those rights are probably held separately. In other words, the studio will have to receive permission from the author of the novel or short story to prepare a screenplay (a derivative work). Add choreography for a film with dance numbers and you have as many as five elements, each protected by copyright. Seldom will all of those rights be controlled by the same party.

In many cases, the screenplay may have been created in a work-for-hire situation, with the screenwriter hired to write the script based on a particular work or original idea. However, some screenwriters are able to negotiate to hold on to the rights to their work. The credits at the end of the film will often reveal who holds the rights. The credits will include, usually at the very end, the copyright notice of the film, which includes the name of the production company, which should hold some of the rights.

Screenplays

Say you have a great idea for a movie script. You spend six months of late nights formulating the plot (and crafting your speech for the Academy Awards). You send off your script and wait by the mailbox for the responses to pour in.

After a few months of disappointment you move on to other things and your hopes of fame and fortune are forgotten. Then one day you hear about a new movie that seems familiar to you, even though you haven't seen it. When you do, you realize that the story is strikingly familiar to that script you had sent to a variety of production companies.

It may just be coincidence. Or, it may be that you are a victim of copyright infringement. And although it is true that putting your work on paper qualifies it for protection under the copyright law, your work must be registered with the Library of Congress before you can file an infringement suit. (As discussed in Chapter 3, just because you own the copyright to the work does not mean you can file suit. You can ask the infringing party to stop using your material, but you cannot bring suit unless the work is registered.)

Registration doesn't necessarily mean that no one else has written a similar story—or that you are entitled to damages if your material is used without your permission. But it does go a long way toward proving that you are the author of your material, as well as establishing when you created the material.

An additional step in proving authorship is registration with the Writer's Guild of America. Members can register their scripts for $10; nonmembers for $20. For forms and instructions, call (323) 782-4500. Keep in mind that this is not a substitute for registration with the Library of Congress.

You can try to avoid problems from the start by including a letter with any scripts you submit. Include a statement that you are the copyright holder of the material submitted, and that you are submitting it for the consideration of the production company or studio for possible production. You can also state that you appreciate their consideration and that if you don't hear from them within a reasonable amount of time you will assume that the script did not meet their needs and will be submitted to other people for consideration.

Theater

A local high school decides to put on *A Young Lady of Property* by Horton Foote. One of the responsibilities of the play's producer is to get the appropriate performance rights to the play. Where does he or she start?

The script probably names the company handling the dramatic rights for the play, which may not be the same party that controls the publishing rights. For example, the publishing rights for *A Young Lady of Property* are controlled by Horton Foote's agent, the Barbara Hogenson Agency. However, the stock and amateur production rights are controlled by Dramatists Play Service, Inc.

The producer must request the rights in writing. The copyright holder will want to know the number of performances, the anticipated number of attendees, and the purchase price of tickets sold. Upon receiving the information and reviewing the request, Dramatists Play Service will then forward a contract with a fee quote based on the specifics of the planned performances. The fee quoted should include the performance rights, as well as rental or purchase of scripts, musical scores, and orchestration.

According to one producer of a community theater, rights fees make up approximately 20 percent of the budget for a given production. And although the cost of the rights is an important consideration, the overall balance of music in the production may weigh more heavily in the theater's decision to sign the contract.

When negotiating rights for productions, one must bear in mind that some contracts contain very specific stipulations regarding the performance of the work. For example, if a theater plans to put on a production of *Fiddler on the Roof*, it must use the specified choreography in the contract for the production.

Another factor that may concern the theater company is the stipulation that rights for a production can be pulled (as close as 30 days to opening night) if a larger production of the play or musical is coming to the area. Although this doesn't happen often, one Chicago area high school was forced to cancel its production of *Joseph and the Amazing Technicolor Dreamcoat* when the musical announced a return engagement to Chicago.

Dance and choreography

Although choreographers frequently copyright their works, only one major case has tested the law as it relates to dance. In 1986, the Barbara Horgan Agency, operating on behalf of the estate of George Balanchine, brought suit against Macmillan, Inc., which was planning to publish a book containing photographs of Balanchine's ballet, *The Nutcracker*.

Although choreographic work is not specifically defined in the Copyright Act of 1976, in the case of *Horgan v. Macmillan*, choreography was defined as "the flow of steps" in a dance. This case involved whether photographs of dancers in *The Nutcracker* infringed George Balanchine's copyrighted choreography. The court cited the Copyright Office, which stated that choreography represents a related series of dance movements and patterns organized into a coherent whole. If a dance is performed, it is not fixed. The steps are danced, then the moment is passed leaving only the memories in the minds of those who witnessed the performance. Consequently, the choreography must be written down (as a script or score), or the performance must be captured on film or in still photos that identify the uniqueness of the steps.

Videotapes

Suppose a father buys a copy of a Disney movie for his child at a local video store. Most people are aware that it is illegal to copy the tape for a friend. But as long as the father doesn't copy the tape, he can, as the owner of the tape, use it in any way he wishes, right?

This issue surfaced in a battle between daycare centers and the Los Angeles–based Motion Picture Licensing Corporation. The MPLC notified some 50,000 daycare centers that they must pay an annual licensing fee (approximately $300) in order to legally show commercial videos as part of their curriculum. Childcare providers and angry parents objected to the licensing fees, arguing that either the center or the parents purchased the videotapes and, therefore, had the right to show them at the center.

Many people apparently agreed. *The Chicago Sun-Times* conducted a poll that indicated that 89 percent of respondents felt that daycare centers should not be forced to pay a video licensing fee.

However unpopular such a licensing requirement may be, the right to control public performance of a work is one of the exclusive rights granted to copyright holders. In fact, most prerecorded videos include a licensing agreement printed directly onto the tape: "Warning! Licensed for private home exhibition only. Any public performance, copying, or other use is strictly prohibited."

After this controversy, a U.S. senator from California considered introducing legislation to exempt childcare centers from paying the licensing fees. However, this proved unnecessary when the Motion Picture Association of America (on whose behalf the MPLC was operating), announced that childcare facilities with 100 or fewer children would be granted a token license for public performance for $1 per year. (The original licensing requirement remains in effect for centers with more than 100 children.)

Speeches

A single speech can provide a variety of copyright issues. A person writes a speech. He or she types it out in order to deliver it as written. Clearly, the written speech is copyrighted as soon as it is fixed form. But what about the delivery of the speech? Once the speech is delivered to its intended audience, it's over. It wasn't in fixed form, so the delivery of the speech can't be copyrighted. However, if the speech is captured on audiotape, then the audiotape is copyright-protected. And if the speech was captured on film or video, that version of the speech is also copyright-protected.

But who holds the copyright to these various forms of the speech? The author of the speech owns the copyright of the words. Does he or she also hold the copyright to the tape and the video? Not necessarily. If the speech was given to the general public and there were no restrictions on taping, then the person who did the taping, whether audio, video, or both, probably holds the copyright to the version he or she taped. However, the person giving the speech may have something to say about it, as did the Reverend Jesse Jackson.

A featured speaker at the 1984 Democratic National Convention, Jackson delivered a speech that was recorded on videotape by Chicago-based MPI Home Video. MPI then marketed the tape, which it titled *Jesse Jackson: We Can Dream Again.*

Jackson filed suit against MPI, claiming it had violated his copyright. Jackson's speech was surely in fixed form (even though he is an eloquent extemporaneous speaker); MPI claimed that the speech was a "news event" and, therefore, not subject to copyright. After testifying in court, Jackson told reporters, "If anyone has the right to exploit the Jackson family for economic gain, it ought to be the Jackson family." The parties eventually reached an out-of-court settlement after MPI was prohibited from continuing to sell the video. Harvard Law School professor Arthur Miller, in an article in *The Los Angeles Times* (August 31, 1988), said that what would likely have been debated in the case was a conflict between Jackson's property rights in his speech and whether he gave up the rights by giving the speech in a public forum (national TV).

Summary

Although performing arts seem to present something of a contradiction when it comes to copyright (how can a performance be in "fixed form"?), certain aspects of performances are protected by copyright. Here are some important points when considering copyright and the performing arts:

©   A performance needs to be "fixed" in some form (video, audio, film, etc.) in order to ensure copyright protection.

©   Motion pictures are protected as audiovisual works. However, the rights can be very complex and are held by different parties. Use the film's credits (when available) as a starting point to identify who holds which rights.

©   The rights to perform a work are often held separately from the print rights for the same work.

©   Most videotapes are licensed for private home use only. Any public performance without permission may be infringement.

©   Speeches may be copyrightable if they are in fixed form (on paper, disk, video, audiotape, etc.). An extemporaneous speech that is not fixed in any way is not protected by copyright.

Chapter 8
Music

T he first major test of copyright law in the new millennium centers around the Internet and the recording industry. Thanks to a college freshman at Northeastern University and a late-night chat-room conversation about sharing music files, a site named Napster was born. The program was written to allow computer users to find and copy music files in MP3 format from the computers of other users. Not only could files be copied for listening on users' computers, but Sony created a portable MP3 player. As if that wasn't enough to give record executives sleepless nights, users quickly figured out how to "burn" (or record) their own CDs.

Napster's defense against claims of infringement begins with the Digital Millennium Copyright Act of 1998, which states that online providers will not be held responsible for copyright violations by Internet users. Next, Napster pointed out that no files were stored on the Napster site. All files were transferred by one Napster user to another. In addition, under the Audio Home Recording Act, consumers are allowed to copy music for their own personal use. Napster claimed that those who access the software are simply sharing files as part of their own "personal use."

Although some recording artists spoke out in favor of Napster (For example, Neil Young stated, "It's great. Whatever gets the music around."), many viewed it as a vehicle that could make music buying a thing of the past. Many Napster users openly stated that they hadn't bought CDs in a long time, because they could get all the music they wanted from Napster for free.

Napster narrowly avoided shutdown by the court several times before striking a tentative agreement with the parent company of one of the parties suing Napster. German media and publishing giant Bertelsmann announced a plan in late 2000 to form a membership-based service that would compensate artists, record labels, and music publishers each time a song is traded. At press time the fate of Napster is still in doubt, but whatever happens, two things are certain: 1) The nature of Napster's file-sharing arrangement constitutes copyright infringement in the minds of many; and 2) the future holds new challenges for the owners of all types of intellectual property.

Musical scores and lyrics

When considering copyright and music, there are many aspects to consider besides duplication. It's important to remember that music is often made up of several components. Lyrics are protected by copyright and are generally considered the same as a literary work, separate from the musical notation, which is also protected by copyright.

Add a new arrangement (the instruments you think will work best, a new tempo, etc.), and you've added another aspect of the song that is protected by copyright. On top of all that, the specific recording of a piece of music may be protected by its own copyright (as we'll discuss in more detail in the following section), apart from the other components.

Even though a piece of music and its lyrics may be in the public domain, a specific recording of the music may be protected by copyright.

For example, all of Johann Sebastian Bach's works are in the public domain. That includes musical notation, arrangements, and lyrics. The Chicago Symphony can perform a series of Bach's cantatas and not have to pay any fees. It can even record the performance and release a CD without paying anyone anything.

Of course, the Chicago Symphony wouldn't hold the copyright to the music, the lyrics, or the arrangement. However, it would hold the rights to its recording of the Bach pieces. Therefore, if anyone wanted to use a part of the Chicago Symphony's recording (on, for example, a CD-ROM about Bach's life and music), he would have to get a master recording license from the holder of the recording rights of that specific recording.

In one real-life example, a corporation wanted to use 10 seconds of Vivaldi's *The Four Seasons* in a multimedia sales presentation. Vivaldi's music is in the public domain, so there was no copyright issue there. However, the version the company wished to use was recorded by the Boston Symphony Orchestra.

When the company requested permission, it found that the orchestra required payment not only to use the piece, but to compensate each performer, plus double the performers' fee for the conductor. Determining that the cost was well beyond the budget, the company purchased the license to use a stock recording of the same music for a lot less money.

Compulsory Mechanical License

How does an artist obtain the rights to record a particular song? What fees does he or she pay? What if the copyright holder doesn't want a group to record the song, for example, because of artistic differences?

Section 115 of the Copyright Act contains a provision for licensing nondramatic musical compositions called Compulsory Mechanical License. ("Mechanical" refers to the mechanical reproduction of the sound.) This provision *requires* the copyright holder of a composition to allow another artist to record the song if all of the following criteria are met:

© The song is a nondramatic musical work.

© The song has been previously recorded.

© The previous recording has been released to the public as a phonorecord (meaning audio only).

© The use of the new recording will be in phonorecords only. (Phonorecords include tapes and CDs, according to the definition in Section 101 of the Copyright Act.)

The fee paid to the copyright holder is the statutory rate, which is determined by the Copyright Statute (the rules and regulations set forth by the Copyright Office). The rate has changed over the years. For example, from 1909 to 1976 the rate was held at two cents. The 1976 Copyright Act raised the rate to 2.75 cents and made further provisions for adjustment to the rate by the Copyright Royalty Tribunal, a committee that meets periodically to review the rate. The current rate is 7.55 cents for the first five minutes of playing time and 1.45 cents for each minute thereafter.

However, although the law makes the provision for the recording of others' material, most copyright holders prefer to sign direct licenses with those wishing to record their songs. According to Donald Passman in *All You Need to Know About the Music Business*, "The compulsory license is almost never used. Record companies hate to use it because the monthly accounting provisions are too burdensome. The copyright holders (publishers) would rather give a direct license because they can keep track of it easier."

Royalty arrangements

A royalty arrangement is essentially a risk-sharing arrangement between a music publisher and an artist or songwriter. A piece of music is like any intellectual property in that it can be bought and sold. The copyright is generally held by the author/composer of a given piece. However, as with written works published by a book or magazine publisher, the recording rights to a composition are generally held by the artists' record company.

Music licensing organizations

Songwriters make money from royalties, plain and simple. A songwriter's ability to make a living depends on his or her ability to collect royalties when the music is played. But how can an artist keep track of every time his or her music is played? Nightclubs, restaurants, bars, and other venues play music night after night. Do they keep track of the songs they play and send a check to each artist? Does an artist get thousands of small checks for each time the work is played in public?

Fortunately for all parties involved, there are licensing organizations that handle royalties for songwriters: ASCAP (the American Society of Composers, Authors and Publishers), BMI (Broadcast Music Incorporated), and SESAC (the Society of European Stage Authors and Composers). The primary function of these organizations is to collect royalties on behalf of their members.

Each organization holds a specific type of performance rights, known as "small rights" (for performance in public places, as opposed to rights to put on a musical production using copyrighted songs). All establishments that wish to play copyrighted music in their place of business must purchase a license from the appropriate organization. The license allows them the right to legally play music from the catalog of the organization from which they purchased the license.

Here's how licensing fees translate into money in the pocket of an author or composer: Various organizations, including restaurants, night clubs, roller rinks, even funeral homes need to play copyrighted music as part of doing business. It would be far too cumbersome to pay each copyright holder each time a copyrighted song is played. Therefore, these organizations purchase a license that allows them to play any of the songs in the licensor's catalog.

©   The licensing organizations collect royalties on behalf of their members, who have registered their works with them.

©   The licensors use a variety of survey methods to determine which works are played and how often.

©   ASCAP, BMI, and SESAC then distribute the fees to their members.

©   The licensors employ auditors to conduct on-site visits to determine when and where copyrighted music is being played, and if nonlicensed organizations are committing acts of infringement.

Recorded music is not the only form of music subject to license. You may have noticed that you seldom hear "Happy Birthday to You" sung by restaurant employees on patrons' birthdays. The reason is that the song is protected by copyright and singing it in a business establishment requires a fee.

In 1996, the leaders of ASCAP found themselves in the middle of a controversy after a letter was sent to some 6,000 children's camps. The purpose of the letter was to notify the camps of licensing fees required to perform any of more than four million songs that are protected by copyright, including such standards as "God Bless America," or even "Happy Birthday to You."

A number of the camps that received letters are not-for-profit organizations, including those affiliated with the Girl Scouts of America. ASCAP never intended to impose the licensing fees on not-for-profits. The intended target was large, for-profit camps, some of which operate like luxury resorts, according to Vincent Candilora, ASCAP vice president and director of licensing.

A major part of ASCAP's mission is to collect royalties from those who perform (or play) their members' music and then pass the royalties back to the songwriters and composers. Although sometimes characterized as the bad guy for "limiting access" to popular music, ASCAP President (and three-time Oscar-winning songwriter) Marilyn Bergman states, "It has always been in the interest of our members to encourage the use of music everywhere—particularly by young people." ASCAP has stated that it was never its intention to bring suit against the Girl Scouts, nor to "license Girl Scouts singing around a campfire."

Irving Berlin, one of the founders of ASCAP, made it very clear how much he supported the work of the Girl Scouts and Boy Scouts of America when he donated, in perpetuity, all his royalties from his song "God Bless America" to them. According to ASCAP, the royalties now total many millions of dollars. "In the spirit of Mr. Berlin, we are seeking to meet with the leadership of the Girl Scouts to rectify the misunderstanding which led to this unfortunate situation," says Bergman.

The director of one chain of camps made his feelings about ASCAP clear when he told his camp directors that they would either pay the licensing fees or start writing their own songs. The director stated that he believed the camps were in the business of building upstanding citizens, and that teaching them to respect the law was a good place to start.

Finding the holders of other rights

ASCAP, BMI, and SESAC license primarily for "small rights." Other groups, often music publishers, grant for mechanical and other rights. And although these organizations don't grant for these rights, they generally know who holds the rights for a given song by a given performer. This makes them excellent resources if you need to get permission for a piece of music.

Each of these licensing organizations has a Web site (see Appendix A) and a searchable database. ASCAP's "ACE on the Web" is particularly user-friendly. ACE is a searchable database of the songs licensed by ASCAP in the United States. For each song, ACE can usually provide you with the artists who have performed it and any other copyright holders, as well as contacts' names, addresses, and phone numbers.

Summary

Although most people are aware that copying and distributing tapes of prerecorded musical works constitute copyright infringement, they may not be sure exactly what they can do with the music they purchase. Here are some important keys to remember when considering copyright and music:

©   It's generally acceptable to make one copy of copyrighted music, provided it is for your own personal use and not for distribution to others.

©   The Audio Home Recording Act allows for the digital copying of copyrighted music. Fees are built into the sales of all blank digital media and digital recorders, which are collected and distributed to copyright holders.

©   When considering the rights to musical scores and lyrics, keep in mind that some parts of a piece of music (for example, the melody) may be in the public domain and other parts (for example, the lyrics) protected by copyright.

©   The rights to a specific sound recording may be held by different parties than those that hold the rights to the music, lyrics, arrangement, etc.

©   Musical artists can record a "cover version" of any song through a Compulsory Mechanical License (Section 115 of the Copyright Act).

©   ASCAP, BMI, and SESAC are licensing organizations that collect royalties through licensing fees and distribute them to the organizations' members (musical artists, song writers, composers, etc.).

©   ASCAP, BMI, and SESAC are excellent resources for identifying the copyright holder for a particular piece of music, or of a particular recording of a piece of music. These organizations have Web sites that make it easy to find the rights holders for the music you want to use.

Chapter 9

Copyright in the Electronic Age

I t has been said that the average American processes more information in a single day than a person in the 17th century processed in a lifetime. Computers are a factor in virtually every aspect of human life, from grocery shopping to visiting the doctor, from choosing a family pet to communicating with your dorm-bound college student. According to the Software & Information Industry Association (formerly the Software Publishers Association), more than 160 million users are connected to the Internet in the United States alone, with 377 million people online worldwide.

The computer boom has created a wide variety of spin-off industries and thousands of new companies. The way people work, play, shop, and communicate has been profoundly changed by the electronic age.

One element of American society that has not significantly changed with the advent of new technologies is copyright law. Although it has undergone four revisions, the copyright law created by our founding fathers to protect intellectual property is still in place and continues to provide the template through which all electronics-related copyright cases are viewed.

But although the fundamental copyright law has not changed, several significant pieces of legislation have helped to shape the copyright landscape as related to electronic rights.

The No Electronic Theft Act was enacted in 1997 following a court case involving pirated software distributed through an Internet bulletin board. Under the act, the reproduction or distribution of copyrighted works with a retail value of more than $1,000 is a willful act of copyright infringement. The most serious provision of the act prevents bartering software in Web clubs. In January, 1998, legislation was introduced to update this act, primarily to allow for reasonable use of copyrighted material for nonprofit educational and scientific purposes, provided that the use does not directly affect the market value of the material. The updated legislation is known as the Collections of Information Antipiracy Act.

In 1998, the Digital Millennium Copyright Act was passed. The legislation addressed three major areas:

1) Online service providers would not be held responsible for copyright violations committed by Internet users, nor would innocent Internet users be liable.

2) Libraries would be allowed to use digital technology for both archiving and interlibrary loans.

3) World Intellectual Property Organization treaties were established to protect the intellectual property of U.S. copyright holders worldwide.

Many people believe that copyright law is "technology neutral." They believe that software, Web sites, video games, and CD-ROMs should be seen as intellectual properties, just as books, music, and other pre-electronic forms of recordation are. If they are seen this way, they are adequately addressed and protected under current copyright law.

Others feel that the law is woefully inadequate—that it is far too limited to address the issues created by an industry that breaks new ground and creates its own copyright issues every day.

In September 1995, a report was issued by the White House Information Infrastructure Task Force (chaired by then-Secretary of Commerce Ron Brown), titled "Intellectual Property and the National Information Infrastructure." The task force's primary goal was to determine what, if any, changes needed to be made in existing copyright law in order to protect intellectual property in the ever-changing electronic age.

The task force gathered information from a variety of individuals and organizations, including representatives from academia, libraries, the legal community, individual creators, and copyright holders, as well as the publishing, broadcasting, entertainment, electronics, and telecommunications industries.

Although the task force recommended several amendments to the Copyright Act, it found the act "fundamentally adequate and effective." Nonetheless, the debates over changing copyright law continue.

Software

As one of the fastest-growing industries in history, the computer software industry has created its own set of copyright issues. Software must be easy to use and easy for users to protect from damage (by making backup copies). Because most programs can be copied to other disks, the temptation to give copies to others or sell copies can be great. Unlike most other media, computer software can be recreated perfectly.

The ease of copying extends the temptation beyond making disks to loading programs onto more than one computer. This is not only infringing but probably breaches the license agreement that limits use to only one computer. Therefore, the temptation can be great for a business to buy one copy of a word-processing or database program, then copy it onto five, 10, or more computers in order to save the cost of buying multiple copies of the software.

However, as tempting as this practice may be, it constitutes a major act of copyright infringement and software piracy unless the company acquired a network license. The Business Software Alliance (*www.bsa.org*) estimates that in 1999, 36 percent of business software applications were used illegally. Although the BSA acknowledges that progress in curbing piracy has been made, this estimate translates into $12 billion in lost business software revenues worldwide.

Site licensing

One method of licensing that is often employed by schools and businesses is that of *site licensing*. For example, a school provides access to a word-processing program as part of its computer curriculum. A copy of the program is loaded onto each computer in the school's computer lab. A site license has allowed the school to purchase the rights to unlimited use of the product within the classroom or department. The school purchases a single master copy of the program, as well as accompanying documentation and then either makes copies for individual users, copies the master directly onto each hard drive, or makes the software available through a network server.

A site license fee for a large organization can be costly, but should ultimately be less than the cost of purchasing individual software packages for each computer.

The details of each site license agreement can vary. Some agreements may involve a single payment, while others may require an annual renewal fee. A license agreement may or may not include software upgrades. An agreement may involve a flat fee for an initial number of copies, with an additional charge for each additional copy.

Manuals are not automatically included in the negotiated agreement, nor are product upgrades. An organization may constitute the "site" in one agreement, and a single department may be defined as the "site" in another. One particular licensing arrangement may require individual users to agree to terms and conditions of use, and another could involve a simple group purchasing discount.

To find out more about arranging a site license for an educational institution or other organization, contact your software dealer (although not all retailers are authorized to negotiate site licenses) or go directly to the software manufacturer.

The Software & Information Industry Association

In 1999, The Software Publishers Association (SPA) and the Information Industry Association (IIA) announced that they would merge in order to form a new trade association representing the software and information industries.

The Software & Information Industry Association (SIIA) represents the common business interests of the computer software and digital content industries. The SIIA has more than 1,500 member companies, including Microsoft, Sun Microsystems, Oracle, Dun & Bradstreet, Bloomberg, Reuters, Adobe, Novell, CCH, and Thomson Publishing.

The SIAA provides networking opportunities via conferences and educational seminars and conducts market research. In addition, the SIIA works closely with Internet providers and corporations in an effort to increase awareness and provide education designed to help those organizations avoid committing software piracy.

Scanners

A scanner reproduces a photograph or other image in near perfect detail, then stores it for future use. More importantly where copyright is concerned, scanning technology gives the user the ability to use an image without decreasing quality.

Images can be used over and over—and even altered. And all this can be done at no cost to the owner of the scanner.

In reality, the cost of this use could be greater than the user imagines. By reproducing, distributing, or adapting a copyrighted image without permission, the user may have infringed on three of the five exclusive rights granted to copyright holders in Section 106 of the Copyright Act of 1976 (see Chapter 2). Some users may claim that their use of an image can be considered fair use. However, the copyright holder may not consider the use "fair."

Scanning and the Internet

Not only can images be scanned and reproduced perfectly, but with the Internet, the images can be distributed around the world with the touch of a key. A quick scan of personal home pages reveals example after example of potential copyright infringement. Images ranging from Cindy Crawford to Dilbert to Winnie the Pooh are used, virtually always without regard to copyright. There are thousands of pages dedicated to particular celebrities or other interests, such as the "Babe of the Day" page maintained by one Internet user.

When the designer of one such page was e-mailed and asked if he had given any thought to copyright, he replied that he had gotten all of the pictures on his site from the Internet and posted them on the Internet, and if anyone ever asked him to remove them, he would do so gladly. A laudable sentiment to be sure, but a clear case of copyright infringement nonetheless.

Scanned images are subject to copyright law. As with copies made on a photocopier (see Chapter 10) or reproduced in any other fashion, using scanned images without the permission of the copyright holder may constitute infringement. When in doubt, ask the copyright holder. (See Appendix A for a list of organizations that can help you find the copyright holders for photographs.) For online information about the issue of image delivery and the Internet, visit The Copyright Website (*www.benedict.com*).

Beanie Babies go to Court: The Fight Over Domain Names

Domain names have become one of the hottest types of intellectual property in the universe of the Internet. In recent years, both individuals and organizations have raced to stake a claim on their own piece of the Internet landscape. But what happens when an individual has registered a personal name as a domain, and a company by the same name wants to use the address for its own Web site?

Consider a case reported in the press as *Giacalone v. NSI and Ty, Inc.* A businessman registered the domain name "ty.com" after his 3-year-old son, Ty. The company that makes those famous plush toys called Beanie Babies happens to have the same name: Ty, Inc. Unfortunately for Ty, Inc., the 3-year-old Ty and his dad got the name first. The boy's father was using the domain for a small business Web site (unrelated to the toy industry) and for e-mail addresses. The toy company contacted him and offered him a very nominal fee for the name. He made it clear that he had no interest in selling the name, because it was named after his son. Ty, Inc. responded by seeking the suspension of the domain name in court. The owner of the name filed for and received a temporary restraining order and later a preliminary injunction against Ty, Inc. Seeing that the courts weren't leaning in their favor, the president of Ty, Inc. eventually paid what the attorneys referred to as "a very, very substantial sum" to purchase the "ty.com" name from the father.

Online services

When people subscribe to an online service and then commit copyright infringement on their home page, does the service bear any responsibility? In recent years, several court rulings have said that providers of online services are responsible if copyrighted material is stored or distributed on their system.

One company that has taken the issue of copyright very seriously is Playboy Enterprises. Perhaps more than most copyright holders, Playboy falls victim to copyright infringement. You don't have to search too far on the Internet to find illegally scanned images from *Playboy* magazine. The company has made a concerted effort to fight back, bringing suit in 1993 against the proprietor of an online service that allowed users to store and distribute copyrighted images from the magazine (*Playboy Enterprises v. Frena*). Even though the service provider claimed to remove illegal images whenever he was aware of them, he was held liable for copyright and trademark infringement, as well as unfair competition.

A similar suit was won by Sega Enterprises, Ltd., the manufacturer of video games and systems. Sega sued an online service provider that had loaded Sega games on its system and made them available for its members to use and copy.

America Online, a major online service provider, has attempted to inform and educate its members about the dangers of copyright infringement, particularly in the creation of home pages. AOL uses its Web Page Toolkit to make home page creators aware that online images are subject to copyright law. There are also independent services that review home pages for those who are concerned about copyright violation.

E-mail

Electronic mail, or e-mail, has become the fastest-growing mode of communication since the cellular phone. According to statistics provided by the SIIA, 75 percent of Internet users expect more people to know their e-mail address than their phone number in the future. And a full 50 percent of users prefer to communicate using e-mail rather than a telephone.

As with most new technologies, e-mail can be both an asset and a liability to users. On the plus side, e-mail is a cost-efficient, extremely fast (compared to traditional mail, which some refer to as "snail mail"), and relatively private way to transfer information between parties.

On the other hand, e-mail users must turn on their computers and log on to an online service in order to retrieve messages. Users also must remember to save messages, or print them, if they want to keep them. Recipients of e-mail messages must also resist the temptation to forward private messages to others, or they may be in danger of committing copyright infringement.

Copyright enters the picture when a person receives an e-mail message, then uses the convenient "forward" feature that comes with most e-mail services. This feature allows an e-mail user to send a message to others, or post the message to one of many collections of messages grouped by subject, such as "usenet" groups. A message can be sent in its entirety, along with added comments from the person who forwards it. However, the ease of sending messages to others doesn't make it a legal practice.

According to existing copyright law, e-mail messages fall into the category of literary works. Literary works are described in the copyright law as "works other than audio visual works, expressed in words, numbers, or other verbal or numerical symbols or indicia, regardless of the nature of the material objects, such as books...tapes, disks or cards in which they are embodied."

E-mail has also become a primary mode of communication in the workplace, and much debate has surrounded the rights of employers and employees with regard to messages created and sent at work. To date, significant court decisions involving workplace e-mail have focused primarily on employees' right to privacy rather than copyright issues (for example, *Smyth v. The Pillsbury Co.* and *Bourke v. Nissan*).

The most important thing to remember about e-mail is that, as with letters, the copyright remains with the author of the message. The sender owns the copyright on the words; the recipient owns the physical space the message takes up on his or her hard drive, or the toner and paper if a hard copy of the message is printed. The recipient does not have the right to copy, publish, or otherwise distribute the contents without permission. So, if someone sends you an e-mail message without giving you explicit permission to copy the message, refrain from passing it on to your mailing list or posting it to a newsgroup. Doing so could constitute copyright infringement.

Multimedia and CD-ROMs

The possibilities of CD-ROM and other electronic publishing seem almost endless. You can include photos and other still images, music clips, spoken words, even video clips—not to mention good old-fashioned text. But as endless as the possibilities may seem, so are the copyright concerns for multimedia publishing.

Now, if you want to expose your audience to the inspiring words of Martin Luther King Jr.'s "I Have a Dream" speech, you are no longer limited to presenting the speech only in written form. You can produce your work electronically. With the CD-ROM version, your "reader" not only sees the text of the speech, but he or she can *hear* the words spoken. Maybe he or she can even see Dr. King deliver the speech. You can even add accompanying music, narration, and other images to make the effect of the message more dramatic. There is no limit to your creativity!

Unfortunately, there *is* a limit to your ability to deliver information—and that is copyright law. Each technological

Multimedia Developers Be Aware!

Multimedia developers should pay attention to the following items when developing their products:

© Contracting with employees, independent contractors, and consultants for the creation of your multimedia work.

© Avoiding infringement of others' intellectual property rights.

© Obtaining licenses to use content owned by others.

© Complying with union rules.

© Contracting for the sale or distribution of your work.

© Protecting the intellectual property rights in your multimedia work.

These legal issues are frequently as important to a multimedia developer as the technological and creative issues involved in multimedia projects. A multimedia developer who fails to obtain the necessary rights to use material owned by others can incur liability for hundreds of thousands or even millions of dollars in damages.

Example: Productions, Inc., created an interactive multimedia training work, "You Can Do It." The script was written by a freelance writer. "You Can Do It" includes an excerpt from a recording of Julie Andrews singing "Climb Every Mountain." It ends with a photograph of Lauren Bacall shown above the words, "Good Luck."

In this example, if the staff did not obtain permission to use the recording of "Climb Every Mountain" or the photo of Lauren Bacall, "You Can Do It" infringes on

---

Multimedia Developers Be Aware! (cont.)

three copyrights: the copyright on the song, the copyright on the Julie Andrews recording of the song, and the copyright on the photograph. In addition, the photograph violates Ms. Bacall's rights of publicity and privacy. If Productions did not acquire ownership of the script from the freelance writer, the company does not have clear title to "You Can Do It" and the distribution of it may infringe on the writer's copyright in the script.

From *Multimedia Law Handbook* by J. Dianne Brinson and Mark F. Radcliffe. Copyright © 1994 by J. Dianne Brinson and Mark Radcliffe. Reprinted by permission.

---

breakthrough adds a new copyright factor for multimedia developers to consider. To present Dr. King's speech in a multimedia format, you need to request the rights to use more than just the words of the speech and the photo to accompany the text. You now need rights for the sound recording, the video image, any music you have added, any additional images you put in, and so on.

I paid for it. Why can't I use it?

Part of the confusion over copyright and multimedia stems from the fact that information (images, music clips, etc.) is so easily accessible. CD-ROM collections of photos, graphics, even parts of musical scores can be found for very reasonable prices at any software or large office supply store. However, as with images found on the Internet, the ease of access to the material, even if you have purchased a collection, does not guarantee that you can use it in your own multimedia project, especially if you intend to sell it.

Software packages, including CD-ROM collections, contain various levels of licensing agreements and should always be read carefully by the purchaser. In other words, you're not just buying the "information"; you're buying the rights to use the information a specific way, and sometimes the way you can use the information is extremely limited by the licensing agreement.

The bottom line for multimedia developers is to be *very* aware. Understand that each component of your product may be subject to the U.S. copyright law. Contact a copyright attorney or copyright professional to be certain that all your rights and permissions are in order. What you haven't checked out could prove to be a costly oversight.

Summary

With new technology comes a variety of copyright concerns. Can copyright law keep up? Should software and other new media be viewed in the same way as a bound book? Or is the law technology-neutral and completely adequate to address the copyright issues of the digital age? Here are some important issues to keep in mind:

©   Even though it may be easy to copy a software program onto many different computers or to make copies, the licensing agreement that comes with the program describes the rights purchased with the program. Using the software in any other way can constitute infringement. Carefully review all licensing agreements.

©   Schools and businesses are finding that site licensing can offer cost-savings and convenience when multiple copies of a software program are required.

©   The Software & Information Industry Association is an excellent resource for education and awareness of software-related copyright issues.

©   Scanning a copyrighted image and distributing
      it without the permission of the copyright holder
      can constitute infringement. The fact that it's
      easy and that many others are doing it won't
      hold up well in an infringement suit.

©   Online service providers may be held liable if
      they knowingly allow copyright infringement to
      occur on their systems. Consequently, the
      major providers are making efforts to educate
      and inform members about the appropriate uses
      of copyrighted material on home pages.

©   E-mail messages are protected by copyright the
      same way letters are (see Chapter 5). The copy-
      right of an e-mail message belongs to the creator
      of the message. Distributing the message with-
      out the permission of the rights holder can con-
      stitute infringement.

©   If you are developing a multimedia CD-ROM,
      be aware of all the rights that may be involved,
      including, music, print, audio, and still image.

©   As with any software package, a CD-ROM col-
      lection of clip art, photos, or music clips will
      include a license that clearly spells out what
      rights were purchased with the product, and how
      you can legally use the material contained
      therein.

Chapter 10

Photocopying

Our lives were forever changed in 1960 with the introduction of the Xerox 914 photocopier. The impact has been tremendous: Businesses and organizations have been able to make copies of important materials—whether one-page fliers or 100-page reports—for employees, clients, customers, and others—quickly and with little cost.

But where does the convenience and affordability cross the line into copyright concerns? Although you may have to make your own interpretations in some cases, copyright law does have some specific guidelines.

Personal use

Say you see a recipe for cranberry muffins in a magazine at the library. You'd like to add the muffins to your holiday menu. You don't have time to copy the recipe by hand or commit it to memory. You take the magazine to the copy machine, deposit your coin, push the button, and put the copy in your purse.

Did you commit copyright infringement? Probably not. The folks at *Ladies' Home Journal* are not out to sue every reader who has copied one of the magazine's pages for personal use. But, let's say you test the recipe and discover it makes the best muffins you've ever tasted. You make 50 copies and insert them in your Christmas cards to friends and relatives.

You now decide to write an article for your local paper on the holiday's best recipes and you include the muffin recipe. A literary agent reads your article, gives you a call, and asks if you have ever thought of writing a book, a collection of favorite holiday recipes. You include the recipe in your book.

Have you committed copyright infringement? What started out as a single copy for personal use has now grown to thousands of copies, distributed worldwide, for which you have received compensation. *Ladies' Home Journal* would have a good case against you.

At what point has copyright infringement taken place in this example? When you received a royalty on the cookbooks? When you included the recipe in the newspaper article? When you made 50 copies and distributed them to family and friends? Unfortunately, the law provides no absolute answers. What is clear, though, is that the copyright owner of a work is granted by law the exclusive right to reproduce or make a copy of the work and the exclusive right to distribute the work. The burden of interpreting the law in each case rests upon the individual making the copy.

We have all made photocopies for our own personal use— whether it be a newspaper article for a research paper, a humorous cartoon we stick on the refrigerator, or a recipe. Whenever we photocopy copyrighted material, it is important to consider the four factors of fair use:

©   *Purpose and character of the use.* Are you making copies of a map to include in 100 wedding invitations? Or are you copying the map to accompany a travel article to be published in a national magazine?

© *Nature of the material.* Will you be making copies of your sister's diary? Or the sheet music for "I Hope I Get It" from *A Chorus Line*? How about your friend's home page on the World Wide Web? Or a love letter from an admirer?

© *Amount and substantiality of the material.* Are you copying a chapter from a 300-page book? Or just a paragraph?

© *Market effect of the use.* Are you copying the Sunday crossword puzzle from *The New York Times?* Are you making copies of an article (rather than purchasing reprints) from *Inc.* magazine to pass out at a national sales conference? Are you copying a software manual for your entire staff rather than buying additional copies?

Archival copying

Does photocopying an article and keeping it on file for future use constitute infringement? This question of archival photocopying tested fair use when, in 1985, six publishers (American Geophysical Union, Elsevier Science Publishing, Pergamon Press, Springer-Verlag, John Wiley, and Heydon) brought suit against oil giant Texaco, Inc.

The suit, which had originally been filed as a class action suit on behalf of 1,600 technical and scientific publishers, claimed that Texaco's research scientists photocopied copyrighted journal articles and placed them in files for future research with no compensation to the copyright holders.

Lawyers for Texaco argued that the photocopying done by their employees was fair use, citing in particular the following:

© The photocopying constituted a goal of copyright—to advance and promote arts and sciences.

© Texaco was not a publisher; no profit was made from the photocopying because the company didn't republish the material or sell the articles.

The case was in the courts for seven years before U.S. District Judge Pierre Leval of the United States District Court in New York handed down his decision on July 12, 1992. Judge Leval acknowledged the fair use arguments, but he found that the ultimate purpose of the Texaco's research was "to create new products and processes for Texaco that [would] improve its competitiveness and profitability." He found Texaco liable for copyright infringement in the case of *American Geophysical Union v. Texaco, Inc.*

In December 1992, the Second Circuit accepted Texaco's appeal. A number of library associations filed briefs in support of Texaco's appeal, prompted by their concern about the effect the Texaco decision might have on not-for-profit libraries. The decision, however, was upheld in 1994: Archival corporate photocopying can be considered copyright infringement. Corporate copiers should carefully evaluate the need to obtain permission and compensate the copyright holder before proceeding.

How does one obtain the permission and compensate the copyright holder? The Copyright Clearance Center (CCC), in Danvers, Mass., is the primary source for a photocopying license. The not-for-profit licensing organization represents more than 9,600 publishers. For more information on the CCC, call (978) 750-8400 or visit *www.copyright.com.*

Classroom copying

More than 20 years ago, the U.S. Copyright Office adopted these fair-use guidelines for classroom copying of books and periodicals in not-for-profit educational institutions:

Single copies for teachers

A teacher may make a single copy of any of the following for scholarly research, use in teaching, or in preparation to teach a class:

©   A chapter from a book.

©   An article from a periodical or newspaper.

© A short story, short essay, or short poem.

© A chart, graph, diagram, drawing, cartoon, or picture from a book, periodical, or newspaper.

Multiple copies for classroom use

A teacher may make multiple copies of the items listed previously (not to exceed more than one copy per pupil in a course) provided that all of the following criteria are met:

© The amount of the material copied is brief.

© The copying is done spontaneously.

© The cumulative effect test is met.

© Each copy includes a copyright notice.

What is considered brief?

© **Illustrations.** One chart, graph, diagram, drawing, cartoon, or picture per book or per periodical issue.

© **Poetry.** A complete poem of 250 words or less that is printed on no more than two pages or an excerpt of no more than 250 words from a longer poem.

© **Prose.** A complete article, story, or essay of less than 2,500 words, or an excerpt up to 1,000 words of 10 percent of the work, whichever is less, but in any event a minimum of 500 words.

© **Special works.** No more than two pages and not more than 10 percent of the words from works that combine language with illustrations and have less than 2,500 words.

What is considered spontaneous?

The copying must be the idea of the teacher (not the administration), and the decision to use the work must come so close to classroom time that there is not time enough to get permission from the copyright holder.

What is considered a cumulative effect?

The copying of the material is for only one course in the school. Not more than one short poem, article, story, or essay, or two excerpts, may be copied from the same author, nor more than three from the same collective work or periodical volume during one class term. There are no more than nine instances of multiple copying per course during one class term.

Course packet publishing

For years, professors created their own course materials for students rather than using traditional classroom textbooks. Course packets—custom packs that typically include copyrighted material—allowed professors an educational freedom. That freedom suddenly came to an end following two important cases.

The Kinko's case

In March 1991, the United States District Court for the Southern District of New York found Kinko's Graphics Corporation guilty of copyright infringement for its practice of copying and selling for profit, without permission or payment of a royalty fee, customized anthologies of excerpts from books and articles that professors selected for their teaching curricula. The suit was brought by seven publishers and led by Basic Books.

Following the ruling, the demand for producing course packets remained strong. Many college bookstores and copy shops took on the role of course packet publisher. Bookstore employees who had previously been ringing the register or placing book orders found themselves thrown into the thick of the permissions process. Almost overnight they had to learn about copyright pages, public domain, and the doctrine of fair use—

all with little or no knowledge of the law with which they were expected to comply.

Professors had to accept the fact that the materials they used were no longer free—royalties for copyrighted material had to be paid. The cost of a course packet rose considerably (more than 50 percent) to cover permissions fees, much to the dismay of the customer (the student).

The court decision was a two-edged sword for publishers. By protecting the reproduction and distribution rights of their copyrighted works, publishers threw a monkey wrench into the already confusing permissions process. Publishers were deluged with requests for instant permission from inexperienced requesters. It has taken several years since the Kinko's case for the course packet permissions process to become more manageable. And although professors are still upset that they have to pay for permissions, they are learning to comply with the law.

Princeton University Press v. Michigan Document Services

On Feb. 12, 1996, the U.S. Court of Appeals for the Sixth Circuit—the highest court to rule on this issue to date—ruled that Michigan Document Services was not infringing on the copyrights of three publishers who had brought suit against the copy shop in 1992 for photocopying copyrighted material for course packets. This ruling overturned a June 1994 decision that favored the publishers.

On April 9, 1996, the U.S. Court of Appeals for the Sixth Circuit agreed to rehear the copyright infringement suit against MDS. The case was originally heard by a three-member panel; it was then reheard by the entire court. Both parties involved in the case were ordered to provide supplemental briefs and present their arguments again. In November 1996 the entire Sixth Circuit vacated the decision of the three-judge panel and affirmed the District Court decision that MDS infringed the plaintiff's

copyright. However, the court concluded that MDS did not
willfully infringe the plaintiff's copyright.

Libraries and photocopying

Other institutions are faced with similar issues regarding
photocopying. Libraries have had to find a delicate balance
between their patrons' demands for instant information and
the observance of the copyright law.

Section 108 of the Copyright Act addresses reproduction
by libraries and archives. Libraries are permitted to reproduce and distribute no more than one copy of a work as long as
the following criteria are met:

©   The copy becomes the property of the user.

©   The copy must contain a notice of copyright as
     specified in Section 108(a).

©   The library has no reason to believe that the
     patron's use is not a fair use of the material.

©   The library prominently displays, at the place
     where orders for copies are placed and on the or-
     der form itself, a warning in accordance with a
     regulation developed by the Register of Copyrights.

(For more information on libraries and copyright issues,
see Chapter 13.)

Copy shops

Ask a clerk at a copy shop to make several copies of an
article from *Newsweek* and your attention may be directed to
a sign posting a copyright warning. Or ask the clerk to enlarge
a *Far Side* cartoon into a poster and you may be asked to show
your letter of permission. Many copy shops have strict policies—perhaps not so much out of respect for copyright as out
of fear of litigation. Nonetheless, having the patron make the
copy at the self-service machine takes away the liability of the

shop. Remember that in the Kinko's case, it wasn't the professors who were sued. It was the copy shop.

Summary

As fast and easy as photocopying may be, the right to reproduce material is one of the exclusive rights of a copyright holder. Here are some important things to remember when photocopying copyrighted material.

© Making a single photocopy of an article, a poem, or a recipe for your personal use is generally accepted as fair use. The more copies you make, the greater your risk of committing infringement.

© In the Texaco case, a federal appeals court decided that archival photocopying for business use constituted copyright infringement.

© The U.S. Copyright Office has adopted a set of fair use guidelines for classroom copying for both single copying for teachers and multiple copies for classroom use.

© Although professors enjoyed the freedom to create their own course packets via photocopying at one time, the Kinko's and Michigan Document Services cases found the practice to be an act of copyright infringement.

© Section 108 of the Copyright Act of 1976 provides specific guidelines for photocopying by librarians for patrons.

© Copy shops have become increasingly sensitive to copyright infringement as a result of the court cases discussed in this chapter. The responsibility is now placed with the consumer, as most copy shops will not allow their staff to make copies of copyrighted material without written permission from the copyright holder.

Chapter 11
Using Other People's Property

I magine a term paper without footnotes or references—a paper based purely on the opinion of the author. Think about how would you feel if you were looking through an art book that merely wrote about the artists and *described* the works of fine art they had created, with no reproduction of *The Blue Guitarist*, for example, to depict Pablo Picasso's Blue Period.

There would be a void, something missing. You would probably feel unsatisfied. Wouldn't you be curious about how the author of the term paper came to the conclusions he or she presented in his paper? Or how Picasso's sadness came through in his art? There would be no depth to the presentations. Using other people's work to explain our own gives our work credibility and substance. By incorporating other materials we add dimension.

Let's say you have been selected to give a speech at a fundraising event for Sudden Infant Death Syndrome. You've found an article written by a mother who recently lost her son to SIDS. You want to use something from the article in your speech. It will be more powerful than the lists of statistics you have gathered.

You have some choices if you want to include the material. You could *paraphrase* the article—tell in your own words what the mother went through. You could *plagiarize*—tell her story as if *you* had written the article (as if *you* had lost a son). Or you could *request permission* to include passages from the article and let the mother tell her story in her words.

Paraphrasing

Paraphrasing is a way to share someone else's story without infringing upon or "stealing" their intellectual property. The key to paraphrasing is relating the material in your own words. If someone held the original material and yours next to each other, there should be a distinct difference in the way each is written. For example, if you were preparing the SIDS speech, you might say, "A mother who recently lost her 9-month-old son to SIDS says that the hardest thing for her to accept was that she might have been able to save him if she had just been there when he was sleeping." None of these words are taken directly from the article.

Plagiarism

The term comes from the Latin word *plagium*, meaning kidnapping. It has been said that the Roman poet Martial accused those who stole his words of "plagium." Plagiarism is the act of taking someone else's ideas, writings, or intellectual property and presenting them as your own.

Plagiarism can be a costly act. Think of what plagiarism did for Senator Joe Biden's presidential bid in 1988 when he borrowed a moving soliloquy from British Labor Party leader Neil Kinnock with no attribution to Kinnock. The act of plagiarism cost him any hope of becoming president.

Be aware that plagiarism and copyright infringement are two distinct acts. Plagiarism is wrong based on ethical rather than legal definitions. Copyright infringement is an illegal act. While an act of plagiarism may also be an act of copyright infringement, only the copyright infringement is punishable by law (as a general matter, infringement isn't a criminal act; *civil* liability may be imposed). If a student takes the words of Thomas Jefferson—which are in the public domain—he or she is guilty of plagiarism but not copyright infringement.

Permission

If you borrow material directly from another source and it is not in the public domain (see Chapter 3) and the use of the material cannot be considered fair use (see this chapter as well as Chapter 4), then you will probably need to request permission. Using copyrighted material without permission, even if you attribute it to the proper source, can be copyright infringement. For example, if you were to excerpt parts of the article on SIDS and include them in an article you were writing on the grieving process—and you didn't obtain permission—the author may have a good case for copyright infringement.

Whenever you borrow material from another source, think about the way you are using it. Have you merely restated the material in your own words? Have you forgotten to cite your source? Does it appear as though this was your idea or word? Will you be using exact words from the material? Be aware that the *only* way to safely use copyrighted material is to request and get permission. A common mistake many people make is to assume that citing the source is all that is necessary.

Material in the public domain

Material in the public domain is free for all to use in any way they wish to use it. You will need to consider the following questions to determine if the material is in the public

Using Copyrighted Materials Safely

Plagiarism, infringement, ethical violations, lawsuits. At times it may seem nearly impossible to use copyrighted material without committing some type of legal offense. Here's an overview of the safest ways to use the works of others:

1. **Paraphrase.** Put it in your own words. Read the material, even take notes, and then write it in your own words.

2. **Find similar material in the public domain.** Find something out of copyright or published by the government that would be in the public domain. You can borrow freely without danger of infringement.

3. **Get permission.** Although copyright holders can say no, they frequently don't. Many will be delighted to have their work exposed.

domain. If the answer to any of the questions is yes, then the material is in all likelihood in the public domain.

©   Has the copyright expired?

©   Is the material from a U.S. government document or from materials published by the Government Printing Office?

©   Is the speech given by a public official as part of his or her job?

©   Was the material common knowledge or common facts?

It is important that you carefully consider the material you want to use, keeping in mind the nuances of the law.

Under the old law (pre-1978), copyright protection began upon publication with a valid copyright notice. That means that a poem by Emily Dickinson written in 1914 (more than 75 years ago) is not automatically in the public domain. Many of Emily Dickinson's unpublished poems were found in a trunk by a relative and not "published" until the 1950s when Harvard University Press released an anthology, *The Complete Poems of Emily Dickinson,* edited by Thomas H. Johnson.

Be cautious of old works that have been translated or retold when considering the copyright status. The translation or retelling may be in copyright and require permission. For example, *The Metamorphosis* by Franz Kafka was published in 1915 and is in the public domain. However, it was translated into English in 1948. That translation was registered, and copyright was renewed in 1975. Therefore, the translation is still in copyright.

Beware, also, of public domain works that have introductory material, editorial notes, or changes. The new material added to the work may be in copyright. Consider the Riverside Shakespeare version of the play *Macbeth.* Although William Shakespeare wrote the play centuries ago, the copyright to the introduction and the footnotes is controlled by Houghton Mifflin, the publisher of the Riverside edition. If you are using any of the footnotes or introductory material, you will have to get permission.

If you have determined that the material you want to use is not in the public domain, your next step is to determine if you can claim fair use.

Claiming fair use

Fair use is without a doubt the most confusing aspect of copyright law. There are no absolute definitions in the Copyright Act of 1976; there is only a set of guidelines. When determining if the use you are proposing is a fair use, you will need to hold it up to Section 107, the Fair Use Doctrine. Ask your-self the following questions:

© What are the *purpose and character* of my use?

© What is the *nature* of the material I want to use?

© *How much and how substantial* is the portion I want to use in relation to the work as a whole?

© What is the *effect* of my use on the market for or value of the work?

If you are using the photo of Whoopi Goldberg in a bath-tub of milk taken by Annie Liebovitz to sell your new line of bathroom fixtures, you may want to reconsider moving ahead without getting permission. Ms. Liebovitz (and Ms. Goldberg, for that matter) may not think it would be fair for you to use the photograph for that *purpose*.

If you want to include passages from your sister's diary in a novel you are writing, you may find your sister quite dis-tressed, due to the private *nature* of the diary.

If you are thinking of singing the first two verses of "Bridge Over Troubled Water" by Paul Simon and Art Garfunkel to market your bridge-building consulting company, you may find yourself in troubled waters. Two verses is a *considerable amount* of the famous song.

If you make 30 copies for your book club of Hemingway's short story "Hills Like White Elephants," you may find that publisher Charles Scribner's Sons could cite a loss of royalty income from the lost sales as the adverse *effect* the copying had on their property.

Caution should always be exercised before claiming fair use with certain forms of copyrighted material. Song lyrics, poetry, and drama are especially sensitive because of their "compact expression." A line of poetry, for example, can be loosely equated to a chapter in a book. What may seem like a small amount of material is really quite substantial. Consider 55 words. While 55 words from the James Michener's *Alaska* is a small portion of the more than 300,000 words that make up the novel, 55 words of Robert Frost's poem "Stopping by Woods on a Snowy Evening" is a substantial amount of the work—more than half.

Any time you adapt copyrighted material without permission, you are taking a risk. Remember that copyright law and the fair use doctrine are written in broad language and meant to be open to interpretation. The only true test of whether a use is fair would be determined in court. Would it be worth the time and money you would give up to defend your position in court? Even if you won? Give careful consideration before claiming fair use. When in doubt, don't. Ask for permission.

Obtaining permission

Once you have decided that the material you want to use is *not* in the public domain and you feel the use is not a fair use, you must obtain permission to use the material. The following steps need to be taken to obtain permission for copyrighted material:

© Locate the permission grantor.

© Put your request in writing. Send a letter that states very clearly what you wish to use and how you wish to use it.

© Allow enough time for a response—at least two to three months. Permissions departments are very busy.

© Follow the stipulations of the agreement you receive.

Locate the permission grantor

The permission grantor is the party who holds the granting rights for the copyrighted material. The granting rights are determined by the contractual agreement the copyright holder has with the publisher or producer of the work. For example, let's say you want to use a chapter from Stephen

King's novel *It* as part of a book on writing. Although King retains the copyright to all his novels, as is the industry standard for fiction writers, he probably has conveyed to his publisher, Viking Penguin, the publishing rights, one of which is the right to license others to make derivative works, such as your book on writing.

I don't envision Stephen King's mailbox filled with letters requesting permission to use his work. Mr. King has more important things to do with his time—such as write more books. Rather, a request for permission should be sent to the permissions department at Penguin USA, the division of Viking Penguin that controls the granting rights for Stephen King's work.

There are instances where the copyright holder does grant permission. Many freelance photographers and writers grant their own permissions. It just depends on their contractual arrangement.

Sometimes the permissions process can get very complicated. Sometimes you can't even find the copyright holder. What do you do in the case where you have tried and tried and come up with nothing? Let's say the essay you want to use came from a magazine published in the 1970s. The magazine is no longer published. Because the rights are probably with the author, you try to locate the author, searching every possible resource available.

Can you use the material without permission? You *can* use the material without permission, but it is just that—*without permission*. The author could find his or her material in your book, then come to you to ask for compensation or take you to court. A record of a "good faith effort" in trying to obtain permission does not substitute for written permission.

There are many valuable resources listed in Appendix A that are available for trying to locate copyright holders. Keep in mind also that there is no substitute for a helpful reference librarian.

Put your request in writing

Your request for permission must be in writing. Your letter should include the following information:

- © The exact material to be used. Mark any adaptations or excerpting clearly.
- © The work for which you are requesting the copyrighted material.
- © The name of your publisher, organization, or school.
- © The format of your work (hardcover text, magazine article, CD-ROM, video, etc.).
- © The estimated number of copies you will print or produce.
- © The estimated price you will charge per copy, if any.
- © The territory in which your materials will be distributed. Will it be limited to your church? Your city? State? Country? Worldwide?
- © The estimated publication or distribution date.

Always provide the permission grantor with two copies of your letter (one for his or her records and one to return to you) and include a place to sign and date the letter. The grantor may not always use your form, but you have made it much easier to provide a response. If you are sending a letter to an individual, provide a self-addressed stamped envelope. (See Appendix B for a sample letter.)

Allow enough time for a response

If you are expecting to hear back in a week or so, be prepared for disappointment. Although technology has allowed us to send a letter electronically around the world in a few seconds, that doesn't mean the person at the other end will respond as quickly. Keep in mind that some permissions departments receive up to 300 request letters per day. Many requests need to be researched to see who controls the rights. Rights can change at any time.

For example, a publisher sells a title to another company, and with it go the rights. A book goes out of print and rights revert to the author. Although some companies are set up electronically, not all departments have this information available at a key stroke. Publishers don't have a huge library at hand with every book they have ever published, just waiting for your request letter. Allow at least three months.

The copyright holder may say no

Can you believe that someone would really refuse permission for you to include their material in your project? Yes, it does happen, and you may never know the reason. Perhaps the estate of the copyright holder is in litigation at the time of your request, or the grantor does not allow any adaptations of the work and you have made changes. It might be that the author feels his or her work has been used too much.

The copyright holder has the right to refuse permission. A phone call might help to explain the reason or to find a way to rework the material to make your use acceptable to the grantor. In any event, understand that the permission grantor may say no for any reason—or for no reason at all.

One well-known author refused to have her work included in a collection of works from multicultural women writers. She had previously granted permission for her work to be included in such a collection. However, at the time of the request, she declined. She didn't state a specific reason, nor did she have to. She owns the rights to her own material. She can say no.

One of the best-known cases of a copyright holder protecting the ways in which his material was used is of J.D. Salinger, author of *Catcher in the Rye*. Salinger is a well-known recluse. He conducts the majority of his business through his literary agent at Harold Ober Associates.

In an incident reported by *The New York Times*, the loyalty of one of Salinger's fans was tested by copyright law. A college student named Stephen Foskett created a Web site dedicated to making excerpts of Salinger's writings available to net surfers worldwide.

Chris Byrne of Harold Ober Associates e-mailed Foskett a succinct message that stated that J.D. Salinger never grants permission for his work to be used in any way, that he goes to great lengths to protect his rights as copyright holder, and that Foskett's page should be shut down immediately because it was a "flagrant violation" of Salinger's copyright.

Foskett countered with two lengthy e-mail messages citing fair use and describing the embarrassment Salinger would suffer if Foskett was forced to shut down the Web site. He also stated his great admiration and respect for Salinger.

Byrne, having stated his point, did not respond. Interestingly, Foskett came across a quote on the jacket of one of Salinger's books that stated Salinger's belief that "privacy and obscurity are a writer's sacred possessions." Having read these words from Salinger himself, Foskett decided to close the Web site.

No matter how much Stephen Foskett and those who accessed his Web site admire J.D. Salinger, and no matter how many copies of *Catcher in the Rye* and *Franny and Zooey* the Web site might help to sell, Salinger has the right to say no to any and all uses of his work, for any reason or no reason at all. Regardless of the nobility of Foskett's motivation to close the Web site, not doing so could easily have brought a suit from Salinger.

The cost of permission

Fees for reproducing copyrighted material can vary greatly. There is no absolute fee structure in the publishing industry.

Generally, the permission grantor will base his or her fee on the information you have given about the way you intend to use the material—number of copies, format of the work, territory of distribution, price, etc. The fee is also based on how much of the material you will be using—how many notes, length of footage (if a film clip), how many lines of poetry, number of words, etc. In the intellectual property business, the price for the property may not always be what the market will bear, but rather what the grantor wants to charge. Don't be surprised if a grantor charges a high fee for the property with no room for negotiation.

Follow the fine print

Contracts, by law, must be in writing. Therefore, the response to your request letter should be in writing. It is of the utmost importance for you to read the agreement or license to make sure you have the rights you need, as well as to find out what you need to do to honor the contract.

For example, you may be asked to pay a fee on the signing of the agreement. You may be asked to include the credit line required or to get additional approvals such as from the author who wrote the journal article you requested. You may only be given rights for North America.

Perhaps the most important requirement of the permissions agreement is the form of credit to be given to the copyright holder. This credit announces to the world who owns the property. Be sure you properly acknowledge the source. If the grantor does not provide you with a credit, follow the sample provided here:

"How to Obtain the Rights to Copyrighted Material" by Cheryl L. Besenjak in Copyright Plain & Simple. *Copyright © 2001 Cheryl L. Besenjak. Reprinted by permission.*

Remember, grants of permission are legal, binding contracts. Read the fine print, and be certain to follow all the stipulations required.

Summary

The best way to understand the value of other people's property is to consider how you would feel if others were thinking of your property. Chances are, you'd want them to respect it, value it, and ask your permission before they used it or changed it.

Here are some keys to remember:

© When identifying a copyright holder, keep in mind that the publication in which a work appears is often not the rights holder.

© The term *plagiarism* comes from the Latin "plagium," meaning kidnapping. An act of plagiarism may also be an act of copyright infringement, but it is not automatically so, if the material is not protected by copyright.

© The key to paraphrasing is relating the material in your own words. The safest way to paraphrase is to read the material, then put it away before writing about it (and don't peek!).

© If you decide you want to use someone else's copyrighted material, and it doesn't qualify as a fair use, you probably need to request permission from the copyright holder.

© Material in the public domain is free for all to use in any way they wish. Several key items to consider when determining if a work is in the public domain are:

– Has the copyright expired?

– Is the material from a U.S. Government document or agency?

– If the work is a speech, was it given by a public official as part of his or her job?

– Is the work considered common knowledge, or common fact?

© Be careful when claiming fair use of copyrighted material. You are still taking a risk by using material without permission.

© Once you have decided that you need to obtain permission, you should take the following steps:

- Locate the permission grantor.
- Send a letter specifically stating exactly what material you wish to use and how you intend to use it.
- Allow enough time for a response.
- Follow all stipulations of the agreement you receive.
- Expect refusals. Be aware that the copyright holder has the right to say no to your request, for any reason or for no reason at all.

Chapter 12

Protecting Yourself from Infringement

T he best way to avoid the hassles and expense of a copyright infringement suit? As I've reiterated throughout this book, the wisest course of action is to get permission before using someone else's intellectual property.

But what if *you're* the one whose copyright has been abused? First, how do you know if your rights have been infringed? How can you prove infringement? And how can you fight back? That's what we'll explore in this chapter.

Police your copyright!

It's not uncommon for writers of children's literature to browse through the latest textbooks to see if their material is there and, if so, whether permission was obtained. Check out the Web. If you search for your name or titles of your work, what do you turn up? In addition to searching yourself, you will want to:

© Understand your rights under the law.
© Put up the "no trespassing" sign (the copyright notice).

© Register your work. If you have to defend your copyright in court, you will have to prove you own the copyright by presenting a copyright registration.

Proving copyright infringement

Let's say you've discovered, through your travels on the Web or by some other means, that your copyrights have been abused. Someone has reprinted several paragraphs of an article you wrote in a book. Or perhaps a photo you took turns up in a magazine spread. What can you do? What steps should you take to get credit or compensation, or to avoid further infringement upon your rights?

1. Prove a valid copyright.

Is the material original, creative, and in a fixed medium of expression? The best way to prove this is with the certificate of copyright registration for the work. If you take the case to court, you will need to bring this with you. Think of it as the deed to your property!

2. Prove the work was copied, distributed, made into a derivative work, performed, or displayed.

You will need to show these things:

© **Access.** Did the infringer have access to the material? Because published works are offered to the public, it is usually easy to prove access. For example, could the infringer have taken your book out of the library? Hear your song over the airwaves? Rented your video? Proving access to unpublished works is more difficult.

© **Similarity.** Is the copy significantly similar? Have words been copied verbatim? Are there identical characters in the story?

3. Prove that you took the "protected expression" of the work.

What is original and unique to the work? How significant is the material? It may only be one line of poetry or a few bars of music.

Remedies for copyright infringement

1. Resolve it yourself.

You have found someone copying your photo. You want the party to stop infringing on your copyright. You can begin with a friendly "cease and desist" letter. By doing so, you are informing the party of your copyright. The letter should include the following:

© Your name, business address, and telephone number.

© The name of your work, the date of its first publication, and the copyright registration of your work.

© The nature of the copyright infringement.

© A demand that the infringer cease and desist and pay for any damages.

© A request for a response within a certain time period.

Cease and desist letter

November 1, 2000

Ms. Ann Gardner, Publisher
How Does Your Garden Grow?
1234 Main St.
Hometown, IL 60123

Dear Ms. Gardner:

Recently I glanced through a copy of the Jan./Feb. issue of your newsletter, *How Does Your Garden Grow?* I found that a sizable excerpt from my article "Making the Most of Your Mulch" was reprinted without my permission.

I own the copyright for the article, which was written in March 1996 and was published in the June 1996 issue of *Better Homes and Gardens.* The effective date of copyright registration is April 15, 1996, and the registration number for the work is TX-123456.

Because permission to reproduce and distribute copies of my work has not been obtained, I consider your use an infringement on my copyright. I demand that you cease and desist from selling and/or distributing any more copies of the newsletter. In addition, I ask that you compensate me in the amount of $100 for the use of the copies to date.

Please respond in writing to this letter by March 15.

Sincerely,

Rob Mather

Rob Mather

2. Work out a settlement.

You hope your infringer will immediately comply with your request to stop infringing. It may not be that simple, but coming to an agreeable resolution is the hoped-for next step. Perhaps a license with a fee for the use would be agreeable. It would also be wise to include a reasonable compensation for the use of your work. After all, you had to spend time "policing" your copyright. Any settlement should be in writing, signed by both parties.

3. Go to court.

You have not gotten the response you wanted from your notification. You feel you have to go to court to defend your copyright. What is involved in a lawsuit?

©   Who can sue? The party that holds any of the exclusive rights or receives royalties from the property.

©   Who is liable? Anyone involved in the right being infringed upon.

©   How much time do you have to sue? Three years from the time of discovering the infringement.

©   What are you entitled to? What can you demand of the infringer?

  – **Injunction.** An injunction is a court order requiring an infringer to stop publishing or distributing the work and to destroy all remaining copies.

  – **Actual damages and infringer's profits.** The plaintiff is entitled to be compensated for the actual money/royalties the infringement cost in lost sales and other avenues. This is not always easy to prove. The plaintiff is also entitled to the defendant's profits attributable

Innocent infringement?

Is there such thing as innocent infringement? Maybe you should ask George Harrison. In 1970 he recorded the song "My Sweet Lord" on his album *All Things Must Pass*. Harrison was sued for copyright infringement by Bright Tunes Music Corp., owners of the copyright to the song "He's So Fine," which was written by Ronald Mack and performed by The Chiffons. Bright Tunes Music claimed that Harrison copied the melody of the song. Despite Harrison's defense of his innocence—that he did not knowingly copy the song—the court found Harrison guilty and concluded that Harrison may have unconsciously copied the tune. The court stated: "His subconscious knew it already had worked in a song his conscious did not remember... That is, under the law, infringement of copyright, and is no less so even though subconsciously accomplished."

to the infringement and that are not taken into account in computing actual damages.

- **Attorney fees.** If you win your suit, the court may also deem it necessary for the defendant to pay your attorney fees and other costs of going to court.
- **Statutory damages.** These are established by copyright law. The plaintiff does not have to prove any loss, but the work must have been registered with the Copyright Office. Amounts vary depending on whether the infringement is determined innocent or willful. Damages can be as low as $200 or as high as $100,000. Damages also may be remitted if the infringer was an employee of a nonprofit

educational institution, library, or archive who reasonably believed the use was fair. It should be noted that the winning plaintiff may choose between actual damages and profits or statutory damages. He or she may not get both.

Summary

Copyright infringement can be costly—for the holder as well the infringer. If you hold copyrights, it's important for you to defend your intellectual property just as you would your "real" property.

© One very important way to protect your copyright is to police it. Check the Internet for possible infringements.

© Put your "no trespassing" sign (the copyright notice) up and register your work.

© If you discover a copyright infringement, first try to resolve it by sending a cease and desist letter, and try to work out an agreeable settlement.

© If you can't work out a settlement, be prepared to take your case to court.

© To prove copyright infringement has taken place, you must prove a valid copyright, prove the work was copied, and prove that the defendant took the "protected expression" of the work.

© If you win an infringement suit, you may be entitled to an injunction, actual damages, infringer's profits or statutory damages, and attorney fees.

© Infringement can be innocent or willful. In either case, there are legal consequences.

Chapter 13

Libraries and Educational Institutions

lthough libraries and educational institutions are in the business of making information available, the very goals they strive to achieve can create copyright concerns. What copyright issues do libraries and educational institutions face? How do they pursue their mission and comply with the law at the same time?

Savvy library patrons are requesting fast food–style service with regard to library material. After placing an order they want instant information. And thousands of students of all ages are now participating in "distance learning" opportunities, taking courses online or via satellite (and needing articles and other copyrighted materials delivered to them electronically). Librarians are eager to fulfill their mission to ensure access to information for all. But librarians have to look to the copyright law for guidance. In academic and public libraries alike, librarians must find the delicate balance between their patrons' demands for services with the appropriate use of copyrighted material as they develop policies for their institutions.

Fair use
and document delivery

Document delivery can be described as the delivery of books or articles in the form of originals, photocopies, or electronic copies to a user upon request. Librarians often are asked to provide three types of document delivery services: photocopies, interlibrary loans, and reserve copies. The question facing librarians is: What is fair use in the library setting?

Title IV of the Digital Millennium Copyright Act (the DMCA), Section 104, amends Section 108 of the copyright law to allow libraries to store printed materials electronically without permission for archival purposes. However, the copies cannot leave the library in electronic form. They must be in analog (hard copy) form unless permission is obtained from the copyright holder to transfer the material electronically. Section 104 of the Sonny Bono Copyright Term Extension Act exempts libraries under certain circumstances from the Act's provisions for published works in their last 20 years of copyright protection.

Photocopies

Who hasn't spent time in the library making photocopies? In Chapter 10 we talked about Kinko's and the legalities of copying. Does the law differ when it's a librarian doing the copying in a library setting? Section 108 permits certain libraries (the collections of the library must be open to the public or available to researchers not affiliated with the library's parent institution) to reproduce and distribute no more than one copy of a work as long as the following criteria are met:

©   The library makes only a single copy of the same material.

©   The library does not profit from its copying.

© The copy becomes the property of the user.

© The copy contains a notice of copyright as specified in Section 108.

© The library has no reason to believe that the patron's use is not a fair use of the material.

© The library displays prominently at the order desk and on the form a warning in accordance with a regulation developed by the Register of Copyrights.

Interlibrary loans

It is impossible for any library to have all the materials its patrons need at all times. For this reason, many library systems offer interlibrary loan service. It works like this: You request material from your library that it does not have. Your library searches the collections of other libraries within the system. The library finds the material you need and has it delivered so that you can check it out. When you're done with it, you return it to your local library, which returns it to the original source.

The Interlibrary Loan Guidelines, negotiated by the Commission of the New Technological Uses of Copyrighted Works (CONTU), permit loan arrangements within limits. The "suggestion of five" guideline allows for the borrowing of up to five items from a copyrighted nonserial publication each year that the work is in copyright.

The CONTU Guidelines address the question of the extent to which a library may request copies of journal articles for its patrons from another library. The Guidelines suggest that the library is using interlibrary lending (actually document delivery) as a substitute for a subscription when, in any one year, it requests from other libraries more than five copies of articles from the same journal title (from issues published within the last five years). The borrowing library is required to certify that the request is within the guidelines and must retain records of such requests for up to three years.

Reserve copies

Many instructors assign readings to their students but find the materials are not readily available, or that the material may be a small part of a book, which the instructor doesn't want to require the students to buy. Rather than making multiple copies of the material, the instructor has the option of putting the material on reserve for students to read in the library.

The American Library Association (ALA) Reserve Guidelines state that the amount of material that can be put on reserve by an instructor must be reasonable and that the number of copies should be reasonable. What is a "reasonable" amount? Considerations include the number of students in a class, the level of the class, the length of the assignment, and the length of time before the assigned material must be read. The ALA also states that a reasonable number of copies (for reserve) will in most instances be less than six.

The demand for delivery of copyrighted material by libraries is on the rise. James S. Heller, director of the law library and professor of law at The College of William and Mary, explains that librarians are feeling the "tension between providing good service to their patrons and respecting the rights of the copyright owners."

The Association of American Publishers (AAP), which strives to protect the exclusive rights of copyright owners granted under Section 106 of the Copyright Act, believes that the new technologies created after the CONTU agreements allow libraries to exceed the intention of the guidelines. In a statement on document delivery, the AAP criticizes libraries' "resource sharing" and cites primarily "the erosion of publishing revenues in this country, from: lost book and journal subscription sales, lost royalty income from licensing and lost new-product opportunities."

Digital distance education

Technology has radically changed the face of education in many ways. One example is the ever-increasing number of students who no longer need to meet in a classroom. In some cases students don't even have to leave their homes to access higher education options. Students around the world are taking courses online or via satellite. Students meet with professors not only in their offices or on the phone, but in chat rooms and via e-mail messages. What was once a face-to-face interaction between instructor and student may now be characterized by the student seeing the professor on a video monitor or on his or her computer screen. Students send their papers and assignments as e-mail attachments.

Along with this shift in the nature of long-distance learning comes a variety of copyright concerns. Educators face the need to get permission to distribute or broadcast copyrighted materials to students. A professor using material in class faces different copyright issues than one who broadcasts the same material to 40 students around the world via satellite. For librarians, questions arise about how to legally make available the required readings students will need. Copyright holders face massive distribution of their works to students, at times without permission or compensation.

The U.S. Copyright Office released a report on digital distance education that can be accessed on its Web site (*lcweb.loc.gov/copyright/disted*).

Libraries and technology

As the digital environment we now live in continues to develop and current law is revised to accommodate the new technology, librarians and the publishing community may be at odds. As the issues of fair use in a digital age are being explored, Professor Heller reminds us that the current Copyright Act is "technology neutral." It makes no distinction between a "hard" or "electronic" copy.

Meanwhile, he suggests that librarians find a "safe harbor" in the law and the guidelines: Be certain that only one copy is provided for a patron (if a copy has been faxed or scanned, the copy created for faxing or scanning must be destroyed or deleted), stay within the CONTU guidelines of the "suggestion of five" for interlibrary loan materials, and observe the ALA Reserve Guidelines.

Educators and their special issues

Although the copyright law was written for "the advancement of learning in the arts and sciences," we must remember that the creation and distribution of information is big business. And whether an institution's goals are to advance learning, to further the public good, or even to make money, respect for the law as it relates to intellectual property must be maintained. How do educational institutions walk this fine line?

Academic fair use

How can you advance learning if you hold tight the reins on material to learn from? How can you learn about dramatic irony if you can't quote from David Mamet or Harold Pinter? How can you come to understand the intricacies of a fugue if you've never listened to a Bach concerto? How can you see the difference between false advertising and fair competition if you can't see and discuss advertisements?

Can a professor bring in a cigarette advertisement and point out to students how the advertiser is enticing children to want to try cigarette smoking? The teacher certainly has the right, through the First Amendment, to show the students the ad and talk about it. He or she may even have the right, according to the guidelines for classroom copying, to make and distribute a copy of the ad to students for this one class. But if he or she reprints the ad in a textbook, there is danger of infringement. Certainly, permission would be needed to include the ad in a textbook written and published for commercial gain. And permission is likely to be denied if the ad and company are shown in a negative light. It would be hard to prove academic fair use in the purest sense of the term in this case.

Let's consider another scenario: As part of a scholarly article, a professor compares Madonna's lyrics from her song "Material Girl" with those of "Diamonds are a Girl's Best Friend." An author now wants to include the article in an anthology for freshman rhetoric courses. The permissions researcher working on the project notifies the publisher that permission will need to be obtained for the lyrics included in the article.

The lyrics will no doubt be costly, and the researcher is concerned that the permission may be denied. She is a little concerned about the way that Madonna has been portrayed in the article. The editor does not see why she can't use the material without permission. The author of the article apparently did not get permission. And besides, she thinks, *What does Madonna care? She has plenty of money.*

Of course, this is one of those tricky copyright situations. What may be considered academic fair use in a scholarly article may not hold up in court when it comes to including the lyrics in a commercial college anthology selling 30,000 copies. Perhaps the biggest concern is whether you'd want to go to court against Madonna and defend your position of fair use.

Multimedia fair use guidelines

"Multimedia," a now-common term in the classroom, refers to the use of more than one medium (print, audio, computer, video) to make a presentation. Students who were once limited to typewriters and carbon paper to create their research papers are now able to use video and computer equipment to create presentations that their parents would never have imagined possible. Educators have access to the same tools as students to make their own classroom presentations come alive.

But, as we have discussed repeatedly, the use of new technologies is accompanied by a new set of copyright concerns. Can a professor create a sampling of rock music to illustrate the history of rock and roll to his music appreciation classes? Can a student create a documentary on teen drug abuse for a sociology class and then sell the work to a company that produces educational videos?

A group of educators and copyright owners, meeting as the Fair Use Guideline Development Committee, has worked to address these issues. More than 50 organizations representing interest groups, including copyright users and copyright owners, brought their views to the table. The group's goal was to address an important question: What is fair use in an educational multimedia environment?

The fair use doctrine suggests that greater rights (free speech, for example) may allow the use of copyrighted works when the use is "for purposes such as criticism, comment, news reporting, teaching (including multiple copies for classroom use), scholarship or research." How far and to what extent can you interpret these words in the law? What is criticism? What is scholarship? Exactly what is educational multimedia fair use?

In 1996, the Educational Multimedia Fair Use Guidelines Development Committee put the finishing touches on such guidelines. The guidelines were debated during the span of the two years that the Conference on Fair Use (CONFU) met, but consensus was not able to be reached between copyright owners and copyright users. Following are highlights from the guidelines:

Permitted educational uses

© *Educators* may perform and display their multimedia projects (which incorporate copyrighted works) as part of the curriculum-based instruction to students in face-to-face instruction, as assignments to students for directed self-study, or for remote instruction if the educational institution provides technology that limits access to students enrolled in the course and prevents making copies of copyrighted material. (The guidelines provide more limited use if copying cannot be prevented.) Educators can also use the projects in presentations to their peers at workshops or conferences and can be part of their professional portfolio.

© *Students* may perform and display their multimedia projects (which incorporate copyrighted works) in the course they were created for and may use them in their portfolio as examples of their academic work.

Limitations

© **Time.** A period of up to two years after the first instructional use with a class. Use beyond two years, even for educational purposes, requires permission from the copyright owners.

© **Portion:**

- **Motion media.** Up to 10 percent or three minutes, whichever is less.

- **Text material.** Up to 10 percent or 1,000 words, whichever is less. An entire poem of less than 250 words, but no more than three poems by one poet, or five poems by different poets from an anthology. For poems of greater length, 250 words may be used but no more than three excerpts by a poet, or five excerpts by different poets in a single anthology.

- **Music, lyrics, and music video.** Up to 10 percent, but no more than 30 seconds from an individual work. No changes can be made to the basic melody or the character of the work.
- **Illustrations and photographs.** No more than five images by an artist or photographer. When using photos and illustrations from collective works, no more than 10 percent or 15 images, whichever is less.
- **Numerical data sets.** Up to 10 percent or 2,500 fields or cell entries from a copyrighted database or data table, whichever is less.

Copying and distribution

Only a limited number of copies of the project can be made. No more than two copies, only one of which can be placed on reserve for students to read or copy. One additional copy can be made for archival/preservational purposes.

When permission is required

The guidelines state that permission is required when the project is used for commercial reproduction and distribution, and also when the duplication and distribution of the projects exceeds the limitations outlined in the guidelines.

Accessing the guidelines

Full text of the guidelines, plus a list of those who developed and endorse the guidelines, is available as part of the Final Report to the Committee on the Conclusion of the Conference on Fair Use (November 1998). The report can be accessed at *www.uspto.gov/web/offices/dcom/olia/confu/*.

Summary

As technology continues to make access to information from libraries and education institutions easier and faster, both must walk the fine line between providing what "consumers" want, while complying with copyright law. Here are some important points when considering copyright in a library or educational setting:

©   Document delivery is described as the delivery of books or articles in the form of originals, photocopies, or electronic copies to a user upon request.

©   Guidelines permit instructors to put a limited amount of material on reserve for their students to review in the library.

©   According to Section 108 of the copyright law, a librarian can make and distribute no more than *one* copy of a work, so long as a specific set of criteria are met.

©   Copyright law is more liberal for those in a purely academic setting. However, the closer the use gets to being a profit-making venture, the greater the risk of an infringement suit.

©   A set of guidelines to help students and educators in determining fair use when working with multimedia in an educational setting has been prepared.

Chapter 14
The Future of Copyright

T he fundamental principles of copyright will remain constant. The law will continue to protect the rights of copyright holders. But as our world and technology evolve, our copyright law will continue to adapt to changing circumstances. Three areas can be identified as those that will have the most influence on the copyright landscape in the 21st century:

© Technology
© Education
© Legislation

Technology

Computers, software, modems and online services, multimedia, and other aspects of technology become more a part of the fabric of society each day. Although technology has increased our ability to create, store, and distribute information, it has also created copyright issues that were unimaginable to most people as recently as the late 1970s.

The greatest tool ever created for the transfer of information, the Internet continues to transform the way we work, play, and live on a daily basis. But the Internet makes it so easy to access, store, and transfer data worldwide that infringement can be committed with a single keystroke. Consequently, the Internet remains at the center of an ongoing controversy and debate over the need for new laws and regulations.

On one side of the debate are those who feel that the Internet is a tool to be used to allow free access to information for all people. Many see no need for regulating the distribution of information. Among those clearly in this camp are those who use sites such as *Napster.com,* people who firmly believe that because they can get millions of songs for free, they should never have to pay for music again. So-called "copyright minimalists" write articles about "copyright maximalists" who they believe want to stop the free-flow of information now available to anyone with a computer and a modem. (One fascinating thing about those who believe in the "free-flow" of information is that they often include a notice on their Web sites telling all who visit that they must get permission before using anything they have created.)

On the other side are those who feel that the Internet must be regulated in order to protect the value of intellectual property. To use the Napster example again, those on this side of the debate include the music artists who make their living on the royalties they receive from the sale of their music. These artists are understandably threatened by the comments of consumers who boast about how long it has been since they bought a CD because they can now get all the music they want free online. Many voices on the "maximalist" side are calling for new ways to ferret out and further restrict illegal copying and distribution of copyrighted material.

In Chapter 9 we discussed the growing controversy over the transfer of copyrighted material in a variety of ways, frequently without permission of the copyright holder. This practice is clearly employed by millions of computer users worldwide. However, this hasn't stopped copyright holders

Please don't sue me!

The following "copyright notice" came from a real Web site. The person trying to protect his material seems a bit unclear about the concepts of copyright and permission.

"I do not have official copyright to the images found on this site. These images belong to the artists. I am using them without permission (although in a non-profit, free publicity sort of way...please don't sue me!). However, the buttons, bars, icons, and other parts of the site do belong to me. This means that you may not alter my work or post it on the Internet without permission. These are for your own personal use only, unless I give you written permission to do otherwise. And not knowing the owner of an image is not an excuse to use it without permission!"

from identifying and attempting to shut down those sites that use or distribute copyrighted material without permission.

The Internet is not the only temptation for potential infringers. It seems that each time you receive a new catalog from an electronics retailer, there is a new product that makes it easy for you to ignore copyright law. Take for instance, "Snappy," the computer chip that can "grab" a frame of any video or television show and create a snapshot of it for you to do with as you wish. The ad for Snappy makes no mention of the danger of using copyrighted images.

You don't even need to be among the computer literate to see the effects of technology on copyright. You can just go to your local bakery. Imaging machines are now available that allow you to put any image directly onto a cake. So if you want Anakin Skywalker, Bart Simpson, or Brett Favre on your child's birthday cake (all without permission of course), just bring in a photo. The bakery employee does the rest. When asked what they do about copyright, an employee of one bakery commented enthusiastically, "Oh, it copies just right!"

Education

Of course, one of the best ways to avoid infringement and increase awareness of the value of intellectual property is education. The Association of American Publishers (AAP) employs copyright professionals who conduct copyright education seminars and distribute educational materials.

There has also been discussion about an effort to begin teaching copyright in elementary schools. It is hard to imagine a better way to avoid copyright infringement than to teach children at a young age that intellectual property has value. Not only can children learn to respect the property of others, they may develop a deeper appreciation for what they create.

Copyright education is not limited to educational institutions and government seminars. Organizations such as the Software & Information Industry Association (see Chapter 9) have gone to great lengths to educate businesses and individuals about the danger of software piracy. The organization even offers the Certified Software Manager certification for those who have completed a comprehensive training program. The SIIA makes an important point when discussing the economic benefits of copyright education and compliance: It can cost much less to get educated and comply with the law than to face an infringement suit.

As copyright continues to take on greater importance in our changing society, education should become more readily available.

Legislation

The last few years have been an interesting time for copyright legislation.

Two major changes to the copyright law came to be. As noted in Chapter 3, the term of copyright was extended by The Sonny Bono Copyright Extension Act. And in Chapter 9 I discussed the Digital Millennium Copyright Act.

Although current legislation may not be as significant as that of recent years, lawmakers are still working to fine-tune the law for the electronic media. Of particular note at this time is the review of the Digital Millennium Copyright Act. A requirement of Section 104 of the DMCA was that a study be done to evaluate the effects of the law two years after its enactment. The Copyright Office has posted written comments received for the study on its Web site (*www.loc.gov/ copyright/reports/studies/dmca/dmcastudy.html*).

In the struggle to find a balance between the rights of users and owners of copyrighted material, more issues may emerge. To stay up-to-date, check out the Pending Legislation section of The Copyright Office's Web site (*www.loc.gov/ copyright/legislation/*).

Summary

As we look to the future, we can anticipate much debate, many new developments and a variety of changes in technology, education, and the law. But some things can be expected to remain constant:

©   Intellectual property will continue to have value, and copyright holders will continue to fight to protect their property.

©   No matter how much copyright education takes place, many people will continue to be unclear on the concept of intellectual property and will, therefore, knowingly or unknowingly, commit copyright infringement.

© When making use of intellectual property, the closer you get to a profit-making venture, the greater your danger of an infringement suit.

© Copyright will continue to be big business.

© The debate over what is too little restriction and what is too much restriction over access to copyrighted material, on the Internet and elsewhere, will continue—and will surely grow louder.

© No matter what the circumstance, if you don't own the rights to copyrighted material, you can save yourself a great deal of money and time by finding out who holds the rights to the material you want to use and getting that person or organization's permission.

Afterword

T he debate concerning copyright law will continue. On one hand, people want free and easy access to information. On the other hand, people want their property protected. Both are valid and defendable positions. In the end, whether the law is amended to reflect changes in society or technology, the best way to respect both positions is to become educated and to remain current on the issues related to copyright. Keeping your *Copyright Plain & Simple* on hand as a reference should help you do both.

Appendix A
Copyright Resources

Associations

The American Society of
   Journalists and Authors
   (ASJA)
1501 Broadway, Suite 302
New York, NY 10036
T (212) 997-0947
F (212) 768-7414
www.asja.org

The Association of American
   Publishers
50 F St. NW
Washington, DC 20001-1564
T (202) 232-3335
F (202) 745-0694
www.publishers.org

The Association of American
   Publishers
71 Fifth Avenue
New York, NY 10002-3004
T (212) 255-0200
F (212) 255-7007
www.publishers.org

The Copyright Society of
   the U.S.A.
1133 Avenue of the Americas
New York, NY 10036
T (212) 354-6401
F (212) 354-2847
www.law 'uke.edu/copyright

169

The National Writers Union
National Office East
113 University Place, 6th Fl.
New York, NY 10003
T (212) 254-0279
F (212) 254-0673
www.nwu.org

National Office West
337 17th Street, #101
Oakland, CA 94612
T (510) 839-0110
F (510) 839-6097
www.nwu.org

The Software & Information Industry Association
1730 M St. NW, Suite 700
Washington, DC 20036-4510
T (202) 452-1600,
F (202) 223-8756
Anti-piracy hotline:
   (800) 388-7478
www.siia.net

Books

Association of American Publishers, Inc. *The Copyright Primer: A Survival Guide to the Copyrights and Permissions Process.* 2000.

Brinson, J. Dianne and Mark Radcliffe. *Internet Law and Business Handbook.* Ladera Press, 2000.

Brinson, J. Dianne and Mark Radcliffe. *The Multimedia Law and Business Handbook.* Ladera Press, 1996.

Carter, Mary E. *Electronic Highway Robbery: An Artist's Guide to Copyrights in the Digital Era.* Peach Pit Press, 1996.

Crawford, Tad. *Legal Guide for the Visual Artist, 3rd Edition.* Allworth Press, 1995.

DuBoff, Leonard D. *The Law (in Plain English®) for Photographers.* Allworth Press, 1995.

Elias, Stephen. *Patent, Copyright & Trademark, Fourth Edition.* Nolo Press, 2000.

Fishman, Stephen. *The Copyright Handbook: How to Protect and Use Written Works, Fifth Edition.* Nolo Press, 2000.

Gasaway, Laura N. and Sarah K. Wiant. *Libraries and Copyright: A Guide to Copyright Law in the 1990s.* Special Libraries Association, 1994.

Goldstein, Paul. *Copyright's Highway: From Gutenberg to the Celestial Jukebox.* Hill and Wang, 1996.

Jassin, Lloyd J. and Steve C. Schecter. *The Copyright Permission and Libel Handbook: A Step-by-Step Guide for Writers, Editors, and Publishers.* John Wiley & Sons, 1998.

Johnson, Scott A., Editor. *The Public Domain Report Music Bible.* Public Domain Research Corp., 1996.

Kirsch, Jonathan. *Kirsch's Handbook of Publishing.* Acrobat Books, 1996.

Kohn, Al and Bob Kohn. *Kohn on Music Licensing,* 2000 supplement. Aspen Law and Business, 1996.

Multimedia Contracts. Ladera Press, 1996.

Passman, Donald S. *All You Need to Know About the Music Industry.* Simon & Schuster, 1997.

Stim, Richard. *Getting Permission: How to License & Clear Copyrighted Materials Online & Off.* Nolo Press, 1999.

Strong, William S. *The Copyright Book: A Practical Guide, Fifth Edition.* The MIT Press, 1999.

Newsletters

copyRights© Newsletter
from JLM Unlimited
1841 Hicks Road, Suite C
Rolling Meadows, IL   60025
T (800) 653-7163
F (847) 202-4791
E-mail: lynda@copyrightsnewsletter.com
www.copyrightsnewsletter.com
$99 per year; bi-monthly

The Public Domain Report
P.O. Box 3102
Margate, NJ   08402
T (800) 827-9401
F (609) 822-1638
$395 per year; monthly; focuses primarily on music

Organizations/institutions

California Lawyers for the Arts
Fort Mason Center C-255
San Francisco, CA   94123
T (415) 775-7200
F (415) 775-1143
www.calawyersforthearts.org

1641 18th St.
Santa Monica, CA   90404
T (310) 998-5590
F (310) 998-5594

The Copyright Clearance Center, Inc.
222 Rosewood Dr.
Danvers, MA 01923
T (978) 750-8400
F (978) 750-4470
www.copyright.com

Lawyers for the Creative Arts
213 West Institute Place, Suite 401
Chicago, IL 60610
T (312) 649-4111
F (312) 944-2195

Poets & Writers Inc.
72 Spring St.
New York, NY 10012
T (212) 226-3586
F (212) 226-3963
www.pw.org
Publications, programs, and services for writers.

The U.S. Copyright Office
Library of Congress
101 Independence Ave. SE
Washington, D.C. 20559
T (202) 707-3000
24-hour forms hotline: (202) 707-9100
Fax on demand documents: (202) 707-2600
lcweb.loc.gov/copyright

Volunteer Lawyers for the Arts
1 East 53rd St., 6th Fl.
New York, NY 10022
T (212) 319-2787
F (212) 752-6575
www.vlany.org

Rights clearance companies

BZ/Rights & Permissions, Inc.
121 West 27th St., Suite 901
New York, NY 10001
T (212) 924-3000
F (212) 924-2525
www.bzrights.com

Ferret Research
P.O. Box 9145
Waukegan, IL 60079-9145
T (847) 623-4744
E-mail: info@ferretresearch.com
www.ferretresearch.com

The Permissions Group
1247 Milwaukee Ave, Suite 303
Glenview, IL 60025
T (847) 635-6550
F (847) 635-6968
E-mail: info@permissionsgroup.com
www.permissionsgroup.com

Web sites

American Society of Composers Authors and Publishers (ASCAP)
www.ascap.com
Searchable database of ASCAP music titles and a list of works to which copyright protection has been restored.

Carl UnCover
www.carl.org/uncover
Searchable periodical database.

Copyright & Fair Use (Stanford University Libraries)
fairuse.stanford.edu

The Copyright Clearance Center (CCC)
www.copyright.com

Copyright Information Page (Univ. of Michigan)
www.lib.umich.edu/libhome/copyright

The Copyright Website
www.benedict.com

Corbis Corporation
www.corbis.com
Searchable image database.

Kohn on Music Licensing
www.kohnmusic.com
Copyright law and licensing music for use and distribution.

Multimedia Law Website
www.batnet.com/oikoumene/index.html
Multimedia law firms, software publications, multimedia organizations, U.S. Supreme Court decisions.

National Writers Union
www.nwu.org/nwu
Union of professional freelance writers.

Software & Information Industry Association (SIIA)
www.spa.org
Conferences, networking opportunities, educational seminars, special interest groups.

The U.S. Copyright Office
lcweb.loc.gov/copyright

Appendix B
Sample Letters and Contracts

November 22, 2000   TPG #094CP97
                                          (include on all correspondence)

Permissions Manager
W.W. Norton & Company, Inc.
500 Fifth Avenue
New York, NY 10123

Dear Permissions Manager:

I am preparing for publication with Career Press, Inc., the following title:

Copyright Plain & Simple by Cheryl Besenjak

Publication Date: 12/00	Proposed Price: $11.99
Edition: Trade	Market: U.S. and Canada
Binding: Soft	Language: English
Number of Pages: 192	First Printing: 5,000

We request nonexclusive reprint rights for the following:

Chapter 1, "How to Make the Most of Your Literary Works" from *Value Your Intellectual Property* by Avery Writer.

Please extend rights to all future editions, derivative works, and to special nonprofit editions for use by the handicapped.

For your convenience, you may indicate your approval by signing below and returning one copy of this letter.

Sincerely,

Cheryl L. Besenjak

Cheryl L. Besenjak
Director

— — — — — — — — — — — — — — — — — — — —

Permission granted:

Date: _____   By: _____
                                    Authorized signature/title

Terms: _____   SS# or FID#: _____
                                              Required for payment

Credit line to read: _____

_____

_____

_____

_____

_____

W · W · Norton & Company · New York · London

Contract No. 1529   Career Press, Inc.

Permissions Agreement

W.W. Norton & Company, Inc., grants the undersigned (hereinafter called the "applicant") nonexclusive license to use the following material (hereinafter called the "selection") subject to the terms on the reverse of this agreement:

Title: *Value Your Intellectual Property* by Avery Writer, "How to Make the Most of Your Literary Works" paperback $300

Credit Line: How to Make the Most of Your Literary Works," from *Value Your Intellectual Property* by Avery Writer. Copyright © 1996 by Avery Writer. Reprinted by permission of W.W. Norton & Company, Inc.

Territory: U.S./Canada

— —

This material is to be used, without change, in *Copyright Plain and Simple* (hereinafter called the work) by Cheryl Besenjak to be published by Career Press, Inc., in the English language only.

Paperback: Pages: 192   Printing: 5,000   Price: $11.99
Pub. Date: 12/1/00   Term of License: 10 years from publication.
Total nonrefundable fee: $300

N.B. reference: 094CP97

                                    By:_____
Signature of applicant   Frederick T. Courtright
                                    Rights and Permissions Manager
Date:_____   November 25, 1996

Cheryl Besenjak
The Permissions Group
1247 Milwaukee Ave., #303
Glenview, IL 60025

In consideration of permission to reprint the material specified on the reverse, the undersigned agrees that:

1. No deletion from, addition to, or other alteration in the text will be made without the written permission of W.W. Norton & Company, Inc.

2. Permission does not extend to material from other sources included in our publication, nor to any illustrations or charts unless specified on the reverse.

3. This grant is not transferable and is limited only to the specified edition(s) mentioned on the reverse.

4. No more than 10% of the applicant's work shall be composed of material quoted from works published by W.W. Norton & Company, Inc. and Liveright Publishing Corporation.

5. If any paperbound or other reprint, or revised edition is contemplated, further application for permission will be made to W.W. Norton & Company, Inc.

6. In the event a book club uses the applicant's work as a selection, dividend, or premium, the applicant will pay to W.W. Norton & Company, Inc., in addition to the fee set forth on the reverse, a sum that bears the same proportion to half the sum or sums paid by such book club as the W.W. Norton & Company, Inc. material bears to the entire contents of said volume, or $25, whichever shall be greater.

7. This grant is limited to the publication of the work in the language and territory listed on the reverse.

8. This grant will terminate without notice if any of the terms of this agreement are violated, or
      a. if the proposed work is not published within two years of the date hereof;
      b. if the published work remains out of print for six months;
      c. upon expiration of the term listed on the reverse.

9. The credit for each selection including the copyright notice as provided on the reverse will be printed in conformity with United States copyright law and acknowledgment will be given in every copy of the applicant's work on the copyright page or the first page on which such selections covered by this grant appear.

10. Grantee will pay W.W. Norton & Company, Inc., upon signing, but not later than 90 days from the date of this agreement, the fee specified on the reverse of this agreement, and return a copy of this agreement with payment, and send upon publication one copy of the applicant's work, Attention: Permissions Department.

11. This grant includes the right to sub-license, without charge, the publication or transcription into Braille or other aids for the handicapped, provided such editions are not sold or rented for a fee.

12. If the material is not used, grantee will advise W.W. Norton & Company, Inc. with a copy of this grant for cancellation.

Appendix C
Selected Copyright Law Statutes

§ 102. Subject matter of copyright: In general

(a) Copyright protection subsists, in accordance with this title, in original works of authorship fixed in any tangible medium of expression, now known or later developed, from which they can be perceived, reproduced, or otherwise communicated, either directly or with the aid of a machine or device. Works of authorship include the following categories:

1. literary works;
2. musical works, including any accompanying words;
3. dramatic works, including any accompanying music;
4. pantomimes and choreographic works;
5. pictorial, graphic, and sculptural works;
6. motion pictures and other audiovisual works;
7. sound recordings; and
8. architectural works.

(b) In no case does copyright protection for an original work of authorship extend to any idea, procedure, process, system, method of operation, concept, principle, or discovery, regardless of the form in which it is described, explained, illustrated, or embodied in such work.

§ 106. Exclusive rights in copyrighted works

Subject to sections 107 through 121, the owner of copyright under this title has the exclusive rights to do and to authorize any of the following:

1. to reproduce the copyrighted work in copies or phonorecords;

2. to prepare derivative works based upon the copyrighted work;

3. to distribute copies or phonorecords of the copyrighted work to the public by sale or other transfer of ownership, or by rental, lease, or lending;

4. in the case of literary, musical, dramatic, and choreographic works, pantomimes, and motion pictures and other audiovisual works, to perform the copyrighted work publicly;

5. in the case of literary, musical, dramatic, and choreographic works, pantomimes, and pictorial, graphic, or sculptural works, including the individual images of a motion picture or other audiovisual work, to display the copyrighted work publicly; and

6. in the case of sound recordings, to perform the copyrighted work publicly by means of a digital audio transmission.

§ 106A. Rights of certain authors to attribution and integrity

(a) Rights of Attribution and Integrity.- Subject to section 107 and independent of the exclusive rights provided in section 106, the author of a work of visual art-

(1) shall have the right-

(A) to claim authorship of that work, and

(B) to prevent the use of his or her name as the author of any work of visual art which he or she did not create;

(2) shall have the right to prevent the use of his or her name as the author of the work of visual art in the event of a

distortion, mutilation, or other modification of the work which would be prejudicial to his or her honor or reputation; and

(3) subject to the limitations set forth in section 113(d), shall have the right—

(A) to prevent any intentional distortion, mutilation, or other modification of that work which would be prejudicial to his or her honor or reputation, and any intentional distortion, mutilation, or modification of that work is a violation of that right, and

(B) to prevent any destruction of a work of recognized stature, and any intentional or grossly negligent destruction of that work is a violation of that right.

(b) Scope and Exercise of Rights.-Only the author of a work of visual art has the rights conferred by subsection (a) in that work, whether or not the author is the copyright owner. The authors of a joint work of visual art are co-owners of the rights conferred by subsection (a) in that work.

(c) Exceptions.- (1) The modification of a work of visual art which is the result of the passage of time or the inherent nature of the materials is not a distortion, mutilation, or other modification described in subsection (a)(3)(A).

(2) The modification of a work of visual art which is the result of conservation, or of the public presentation, including lighting and placement, of the work is not a destruction, distortion, mutilation, or other modification described in subsection (a)(3) unless the modification is caused by gross negligence.

(3) The rights described in paragraphs (1) and (2) of subsection (a) shall not apply to any reproduction, depiction, portrayal, or other use of a work in, upon, or in any connection with any item described in subparagraph (A) or (B) of the definition of "work of visual art" in section 101, and any such reproduction, depiction, portrayal, or other use of a work is not a destruction, distortion, mutilation, or other modification described in paragraph (3) of subsection (a).

(d) Duration of Rights.- (1) With respect to works of visual art created on or after the effective date set forth in section

610(a) of the Visual Artists Rights Act of 1990, the rights conferred by subsection (a) shall endure for a term consisting of the life of the author.

(2) With respect to works of visual art created before the effective date set forth in section 610(a) of the Visual Artists Rights Act of 1990, but title to which has not, as of such effective date, been transferred from the author, the rights conferred by subsection (a) shall be coextensive with, and shall expire at the same time as, the rights conferred by section 106.

(3) In the case of a joint work prepared by two or more authors, the rights conferred by subsection (a) shall endure for a term consisting of the life of the last surviving author.

(4) All terms of the rights conferred by subsection (a) run to the end of the calendar year in which they would otherwise expire.

(e) Transfer and Waiver.- (1) The rights conferred by subsection (a) may not be transferred, but those rights may be waived if the author expressly agrees to such waiver in a written instrument signed by the author. Such instrument shall specifically identify the work, and uses of that work, to which the waiver applies, and the waiver shall apply only to the work and uses so identified. In the case of a joint work prepared by two or more authors, a waiver of rights under this paragraph made by one such author waives such rights for all such authors.

(2) Ownership of the rights conferred by subsection (a) with respect to a work of visual art is distinct from ownership of any copy of that work, or of a copyright or any exclusive right under a copyright in that work. Transfer of ownership of any copy of a work of visual art, or of a copyright or any exclusive right under a copyright, shall not constitute a waiver of the rights conferred by subsection (a). Except as may otherwise be agreed by the author in a written instrument signed by the author, a waiver of the rights conferred by subsection (a) with respect to a work of visual art shall not constitute a transfer of ownership of any copy of that work, or of ownership of a copyright or of any exclusive right under a copyright in that work.

§ 107. Limitations on exclusive rights: Fair use

Notwithstanding the provisions of sections 106 and 106A, the fair use of a copyrighted work, including such use by reproduction in copies or phonorecords or by any other means specified by that section, for purposes such as criticism, comment, news reporting, teaching (including multiple copies for classroom use), scholarship, or research, is not an infringement of copyright. In determining whether the use made of a work in any particular case is a fair use the factors to be considered shall include:

1. the purpose and character of the use, including whether such use is of a commercial nature or is for nonprofit educational purposes;

2. the nature of the copyrighted work;

3. the amount and substantiality of the portion used in relation to the copyrighted work as a whole; and

4. the effect of the use upon the potential market for or value of the copyrighted work.

The fact that a work is unpublished shall not itself bar a finding of fair use if such finding is made upon consideration of all the above factors.

Index

About the Author

Cheryl Besenjak is founder and director of The Permissions Group, a full-service rights and permissions consulting company in Glenview, Ill. (near Chicago). She conducts copyright education seminars at The Permissions Group and across the United States. Cheryl is the former publisher of *copyRights©* newsletter, for which she currently serves as an advisor.

Cheryl has woven her active professional life in and around her family and her church. She lives with her husband Joe, daughter Kate, and their black lab, Rebecca, in a northwest suburb of Chicago. Cheryl and her family are deeply involved in the ministry of Willow Creek Community Church.